	Option 1	Option 2	Option 3	Option 4	Option 5
FREE LIFT	may elect to play ... e ball as it lies	Thru green: drop w/in 1 club at a point away from interference, not nearer hole, not in hazard or on green	In bunker (w/no penalty): drop in hazard, nearest to original spot, away from interference, not nearer hole	In bunker (w/ penalty): drop outside hazard on any point on a line from hole thru point of inference to where ball is dropped (1 stroke)	On green: lift and place away from interference, not nearer hole, not in hazard; nearest point of relief may be off green
Cas...	its own pitch-mark be lifted, cleaned, dropped	Only applies thru green in "closely mown" area	"Closely mown" means any area cut to fairway height or less	As close as possible to embedded spot, but not nearer hole	No free lift in rough or hazards (see Unplayable Lie)
Putting Green	all on wrong green MUST be lifted	Drop w/in 1 club at nearest point of relief:	Not nearer correct hole, not in hazard or on green	Nearest point of relief is probably on the apron;	Ball may be cleaned when lifted
Obstructions	Movable (1) Ball blocked by, but not in or on obstr.; obstr. may be moved, if ball moves, replace it	Movable (2) Ball in/un obstr. may be lifted & obstr. removed; thru green ball dropped; on green, ball placed	Immovable thru green: drop w/in 1 club of point of nearest relief; not nearer hole, avoids the interference, not in a hazard or on the green	Immovable in bunker: drop w/in 1 club of point not nearer hole, avoids the interference; must be dropped in bunker	Immovable on green: lift and place away from obstruction, not nearer hole, not in hazard
Pace of Play	Play ready golf; stay within ½ hole of the group ahead of you	Choose proper tees; hit provisional ball if your shot may be lost outside a hazard	Be prepared; use a quick pre-shot routine; when hitting; leave bags at exit of hole; write scores on next tee	Line up putt while others hitting; leave bags at exit of hole; write scores on next tee	Let group behind hit up to green, then putt out

PENALTY	Option 1	Option 2	Option 3	Option 4	Option 5
White Stakes (OB)	Re-hit from original spot (1 stroke)				
Lost Ball (not in a hazard)	Re-hit from original spot (1 stroke)				
Yellow Stakes (water hazard)	Play it as it lies (no penalty)	Drop on any point from hole thru spot where ball entered hazard (1 stroke)	Re-hit from original spot (1 stroke)		
Red Stakes (lateral hazard)	Play it as it lies (no penalty)	Drop on any point on a line from the hole through point ball last crossed into hazard (1 stroke)	Re-hit from original spot (1 stroke)	Drop w/in 2 clubs of spot where ball last crossed into hazard, not nearer the hole (1 stroke)	Drop w/in 2 clubs of spot across hazard from where ball last crossed into hazard, not nearer the hole (1 stroke)
Unplayable Lie (not in water hazard)	Re-hit from original spot (1 stroke)	Drop on any point on a line from the hole through point where ball lies (1 stroke)	Drop w/in 2 club lengths of where ball lies, not nearer the hole (1 stroke)		
Provisional Ball	If ball may be lost (outside of a water hazard) announce intent to play provisional ball	Play provisional ball up to the spot where original ball may be lost; search for original ball	If original ball is found, it must be played under appropriate rules; see above	If original ball is lost, or is OB, provisional ball becomes "ball in play" (1 stroke)	

Golf Rules and Etiquette

by Jim Corbett

ALPHA

A member of Penguin Group (USA) Inc.

ALPHA BOOKS

Published by the Penguin Group

Penguin Group (USA) Inc., 375 Hudson Street, New York, New York 10014, U.S.A.

Penguin Group (Canada), 10 Alcorn Avenue, Toronto, Ontario, Canada M4V 3B2 (a division of Pearson Penguin Canada Inc.)

Penguin Books Ltd, 80 Strand, London WC2R 0RL, England

Penguin Ireland, 25 St Stephen's Green, Dublin 2, Ireland (a division of Penguin Books Ltd)

Penguin Group (Australia), 250 Camberwell Road, Camberwell, Victoria 3124, Australia (a division of Pearson Australia Group Pty Ltd)

Penguin Books India Pvt Ltd, 11 Community Centre, Panchsheel Park, New Delhi—110 017, India

Penguin Group (NZ), cnr Airborne and Rosedale Roads, Albany, Auckland 1310, New Zealand (a division of Pearson New Zealand Ltd)

Penguin Books (South Africa) (Pty) Ltd, 24 Sturdee Avenue, Rosebank, Johannesburg 2196, South Africa

Penguin Books Ltd, Registered Offices: 80 Strand, London WC2R 0RL, England

International Standard Book Number: 978-1-59257-642-5
Library of Congress Catalog Card Number: 2006938604

09   08   07   8   7   6   5   4   3   2   1

Interpretation of the printing code: The rightmost number of the first series of numbers is the year of the book's printing; the rightmost number of the second series of numbers is the number of the book's printing. For example, a printing code of 07-1 shows that the first printing occurred in 2007.

Printed in the United States of America

To my parents, Frank and Lorraine Corbett. And to the other members of my life's foursome, my wife Tami, my daughter, Arcadia, and my son, Jeffrey

Contents

Introduction

The rules of golf are many, they are confusing, and they are hard to find when you need them the most. Many's the time I have encountered a furious golfer standing over a questionable lie with a copy of the rulebook in hand. Madly he thumbs the pages to figure out the explanation of the particular situation in which he is snared. Finally, in total frustration, the book is heaved into the bushes along with a club or two. The golfer whacks the ball and staggers off, a beaten man.

The Pocket Idiot's Guide to Golf Rules and Etiquette is organized to provide the maximum help to the golfer when it is needed most—out on the course. Clearly it is impossible to include every single rule of golf and every etiquette consideration within the confines of a pocket guide (you would need an extra caddy just to help carry the several volumes of such a work along the course with you). Instead, the major rules affecting the play of the game and the important etiquette rules are covered so every golfer from the low-handicapper to the weekend hacker to the once-a-year-corporate-duffer will find the help they need in a substantive but easy-to-use book that will keep everyone playing the same game.

The handy-dandy "tear-out" card with the penalty and free lift situations is something that every golfer should laminate and keep on his or her golf bag as a quick reference tool. It will be indispensable for those all-too-common situations that occur on the golf course but that only a few golfers seem to know how to resolve. Now you, too, can be admired as a font of wisdom and knowledge, and feared as a source of extra strokes by your friends and enemies alike. And soon it will be hard to tell those two groups apart.

The rules of golf and golf etiquette are what define this great game. The history, traditions, and the unique qualities of the game are intimately tied to the rules and the etiquette. So enjoy the game and play well. But to be sure you are playing the right game, take along a copy of *The Pocket Idiot's Guide to Golf Rules and Etiquette*.

Extras

The sidebars in this book will be used to further explain a point, outline a general area, or provide a fun perspective on some of golf's rules or etiquette.

Keeping Up With the Bobby Joneses

Bobby Jones is considered by many to represent the epitome of good golf etiquette. I'll use this sidebar to provide a quick outline of etiquette material covered in a chapter.

Did You Know That?

Many of the rules of golf and etiquette have little nuances or tricks to them that might not be clear from a reading of the rules, so this item will bring some of those nuances to your attention.

The Words and Wisdom on Golf

More than any other sport, golf lends itself to philosophical observations that range from the brilliant to the banal. Plus there are some great terms in golf that may need a little explaining. All of that will be collected under this banner.

Acknowledgments

I'd like to thank Bob Brown, founder of Keepers of the Game (www.keepersofthegame.org); Rick Newell of the cartoon strip, *Life in the Trap* (www.lifeinthetrap.com); my radio co-host Corky Frady; and John Saegner Jr. of the Washington State Golf Association. I'd also like to thank Nancy Lewis and all of the other people at Alpha Books for making the process of creating this book so painless.

Trademarks

All terms mentioned in this book that are known to be or are suspected of being trademarks or service marks have been appropriately capitalized. Alpha Books and Penguin Group (USA) Inc. cannot attest to the accuracy of this information. Use of a term in this book should not be regarded as affecting the validity of any trademark or service mark.

Chapter

Before You Begin

In This Chapter

- Playing it safe
- Attitude, schmattitude—I hate this game!
- Does the clothing make the golfer?
- Golfers come fully equipped
- Measure your potential with a handicap
- Care to join me for tee?

With all of the excitement and anticipation that precedes a round of golf, it is important to make sure that at the end of the day, everyone is still happy, friends, and looking forward to the next opportunity to play. If you follow a few simple guidelines, then the game will reward you with a lifetime of fun, outstanding friendships, and terrific memories.

Before you step onto the course, however, there are a few things on your to-do list that have nothing to do with getting the ball into the hole. But they will greatly contribute to the overall success of your day. How well you prepare yourself physically, mentally, and emotionally goes a long way toward setting the proper tone for a great round of golf.

Practice Safe Golf

The game of golf is hard ... but the golf clubs are even harder. So it's a good idea to keep your head and the heads of all those golf clubs from coming into contact with one another. Before you take a practice swing anywhere around the course or the *practice range* or even around your living room, be sure that no one is nearby and about to walk into a long and expensive future at the *orthodontist's* office.

Did You Know That?

Of all the summer sports camps that are organized for kids around the United States, including football, soccer, baseball, and many others, kids in golf camps sustain the greatest number of serious injuries! Most occur from not watching where they swing the club.

The value of a practice swing is to set the tempo of your swing and to reinforce the proper *swing plane* for your shot. You can do that without ever hitting the ground. And when you do, you avoid two very important *golf etiquette* problems:

- You avoid making a mess out of the fairways and *tee boxes*, and

- You avoid hitting someone else with the general debris that your golf club might scoop up.

An important golf etiquette principle that will win you friends and help you retain playing partners is this: don't injure the people you are playing with. When you are poised at the end of a perfect practice swing, look at your playing partner. If he is spitting out a combination of dirt, broken tees, and sticks, while wiping mud and bits of *divot* off his reflective wrap-arounds, it will probably detract from the Kodak moment you were hoping for.

Make your practice swing an effective tool to groove your shot without damaging the golf course or outfitting your friends with divot toupees.

Golfers: Stretching More Than Just the Truth

Golf can provide a lifetime of fun and enjoyment, but if you are not properly prepared, it can be a pain in the neck—or the back. Golfers sustain lower-back, hand, and wrist injuries quite often. And as difficult as this may be to believe, those injuries frequently occur because the golfer has either not adequately warmed up or has very poor technique—or both.

The modern golf swing, which focuses on strength, torque, and increased swing speed, requires your body to do some things it might not be ready for.

Stretches and strength-building will help you withstand the turning and twisting associated with the golf swing and with the endurance of sustaining that activity over 18 holes.

The Words and Wisdom on Golf

The golf swing is like a suitcase into which we are trying to pack one too many things.

—John Updike

Your body's core muscles (abdominals, obliques, lower back, and hamstrings) carry most of the burden of the golf swing and should be strengthened regularly and stretched before each round. Consult with a trainer to establish a program to get yourself into shape and watch those scores come down.

Unfortunately only lessons and practice will help with your technique.

Fore! He's a Jolly Good Fellow

Sometimes it is possible to hit a golf ball much farther than we realize we can hit it. And it always seems to happen when we least expect it. Boom! That sweet sensation pulses up through the club and reverberates through every cell of your body. Then you think, "Hmmm, I wonder if that group ahead is far enough out of the … *Fore!*"

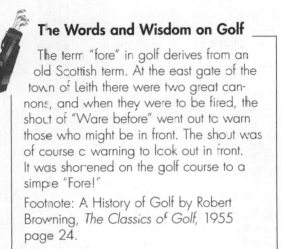

The Words and Wisdom on Golf

The term "fore" in golf derives from an old Scottish term. At the east gate of the town of Leith there were two great cannons, and when they were to be fired, the shout of "Ware before" went out to warn those who might be in front. The shout was of course a warning to look out in front. It was shortened on the golf course to a simple "Fore!"

Footnote: A History of Golf by Robert Browning, *The Classics of Golf,* 1955 page 24.

If you do hit a shot that appears as though it has the possibility of coming near some innocent bystander, take the one sanctioned opportunity to shout at the top of your lungs on the golf course. Holler, "Fore!" That is the golfer's universal term for "duck and cover," and it will be much appreciated by those on the receiving end of your incoming missile.

Be sure to let the group in front of you play ahead to a safe range before you hit your shot of a lifetime. Golf is a great way to meet new people, but the introductions go much more smoothly when you have not just put a big welt on your new friend's back with your golf ball.

Did You Know That?

Depending on where you live, a golfer may be liable for injury inflicted upon other golfers caused by bad golf shots. Check your insurance policy, but better yet, be careful not to hit into other groups.

In the Line of Fire

Isn't it amazing to watch a golf match on TV? You see a famous pro golfer lining up her tee shot and a crowd of spectators forming a human funnel crowded six people deep. They line up about three feet from where the pro is going to launch her hopes at about 800 miles per hour through the funnel. And it seems like every one of those spectators is trying to crane his face right out in front so they catch a glimpse at that ball as it comes off the clubface.

Well, let me take this opportunity to point out a very important distinction between a touring pro and the golfers that you will be playing with. The pros have a pretty good chance of hitting the ball where they aim it; and it isn't clear if the golfers you play with actually aim it at all.

So here is an important safety tip: don't stand in front of a golfer who is hitting a shot! Unless you are looking for a low-cost tattoo with a familiar dimpled pattern strategically located on your forehead, stand behind the person who is hitting.

The Words and Wisdom on Golf

I know I am getting better at golf because I'm hitting fewer spectators.
—Gerald Ford

Lightning Your Load

One of the most satisfying experiences in the game of golf is hitting a nice crisp shot up to the green. But that is the only time you want the word crisp to describe anything related to your golf game. For instance, you don't want to hear about how you were "fried to a crisp" when you got struck by lightning on the golf course.

Many golfers are familiar with the joke about lightning, which is usually attributed to Lee Trevino: when you're out on the golf course in a lightning storm, hold up your 1-iron, because even God can't hit a 1-iron. Turns out that might not be true.

Did You Know That?

According to the Golf Course Superintendents Association of America (GCSAA), as many as 300 people die from lightning strikes in the United States every year.

Some people think that when they see a thunderstorm gathering that they can play out their round, or wait until they see the first few flashes of lightning before they have to hop into their carts and out run it back to the clubhouse.

But consider the following little Internet factoid: lightning is initiated in the clouds and begins traveling to Earth at 200,000 miles per hour; then positive charges in the earth travel up to meet that surge and when the connection is made, the resulting flash that we see travels at 200,000,000 (yes, that is 200 million) miles per hour. Which, as it turns out, is quite a bit faster than the average golf cart.

So instead of relying on your ability to outrun the storm, why not take the advice of the GCSAA instead? Here is what they recommend as reasonable safety precautions:

- Seek shelter at the first sign of a thunderstorm.
- If the course's warning system sounds, take cover.
- If possible, get off the golf course or go to a designated lightning shelter.
- Do not stand under a lone tree. This is where most people are injured or killed.
- Stay away from your golf clubs.
- If your shoes have metal spikes, take them off.
- Move away from your golf cart.

- If stranded in the open, go to a low place such as a ravine or valley.
- Stay away from water (this one is advice that golfers want to follow all day long).

That sounds like it should be Plan A if the possibility of lightning exists. Outrunning the storm in your golf cart is somewhere down around Plan Y. (And just in case you were wondering, the 1-iron in the air is Plan Z.)

Keeping Up With the Bobby Joneses

When you prepare to swing, either for practice or for real, be sure no one is nearby.

When you are walking around other golfers, be sure no one else is taking a practice swing.

Never take a practice swing in the direction of other people.

Exercise and stretching will help build and sustain a good swing.

Don't stand in front of a golfer who is hitting a shot.

Be sure the group ahead of you is out of range before you hit.

Holler "FORE!" if your shot is heading toward another golfer.

Follow the advice of the GSCAA regarding lightning.

Stay safe, keep those around you safe, and you can all come back and play again.

Attitude Is Everything

The two most important components to a successful golf game are skill and a positive attitude. Of course, you can get further with a lot of skill and a lousy attitude than you can with hardly any skill and a dopey grin on your face. But you'll be a lot more fun to be around if you are the latter—and much more fun to bet with.

The Words and Wisdom on Golf

Golf is a game that is played on a 5-inch course—the distance between your ears.

—Bobby Jones

Let's face it: golf is frustrating. It's especially frustrating for a new golfer. And it's really especially frustrating for a golfer who has played for a long time. You've practiced for hours, you've taken endless lessons, and you've paid a king's ransom for clubs, yet you still slice the ball deep into the woods. Then you see some guy who has as much grace as the proverbial "one-legged man in a butt-kicking contest," and he rips one right down the middle.

Stay calm. Take a deep breath. And now repeat after me, "Golf is just a game."

Golf is very easy to play, but very difficult to play well. Once you decide you are going to appreciate the play of the game and respect the traditions of the game, then everything else becomes easier and more enjoyable.

The Words and Wisdom on Golf

Golf is so popular simply because it is the best game in the world at which to be bad.

—A.A. Milne

Golf is also a very social game. Not only are you interacting with the people in your own foursome, but you frequently come into contact with the groups ahead of you and behind you—and if you spray the ball like I do, the groups on all sides of you, as well. Remember, they paid their money for a great day and they may actually be having one, so don't ruin everyone else's day with a negative attitude.

If you keep the attitude positive, you'll play better and everyone around you will enjoy the day and want to play with you again the next time, especially if you are that easy to beat.

Keeping Up With the Bobby Joneses

Golf is frustrating from time to time for everyone.

Approach the game with reasonable expectations.

Your attitude affects everyone in your group.

Provide a good example to young players in your group.

Remember: golf is just a game!

What the Smart Golfer Is Wearing

Most golf courses appreciate it when the golfers all wear clothing. There are some nudist resorts where this is not the case; however, an entirely different level of etiquette is required in order to play there.

In the 1950s and '60s, golf was often ridiculed as "Republicans in bad pants." But looking back at some of the styles on the tour in the '70s and '80s makes the '50s look pretty good. The game has grown tremendously since then, though; and with a much more egalitarian appeal, it is safe to say that golfers of all political parties, religious persuasions, and national origins can now mismatch styles with equal opportunity.

Clothing at a golf course becomes an issue because most facilities try to maintain a high level of dignity on the course. If you are going to be swearing and breaking clubs and throwing things into the lake, at least you should be smartly attired while doing so.

The Words and Wisdom on Golf

Here is the wording of an actual clothing policy posted on the website of a prestigious golf resort: Traditional golf attire required. Gentlemen's shirts must have a collar and sleeves. Shorts must be of moderate length and hemmed. Cut-off shorts, athletic shorts, or running shorts are not allowed. Tank tops, halter tops, tube tops, or cropped tops are not allowed. Denim is not allowed on the course or the practice facilities.

That generally means men should wear golf shirts that have collars (an attempt to avoid the tank top and the whole hairy armpit thing), and avoid wearing jeans or cut-offs. People often ask if shorts are acceptable attire on the golf course, and naturally the answer to that question depends on how knobby one's knees are.

Women have many more fashion options available to them including shorts, skirts, slacks, and a dizzying array of options for mixing and matching their ensembles. I have just stepped completely out of my depth of knowledge on the subject of ladies' fashions on or off the golf course.

The most important thing to remember is that in order to swing properly you will need to wear something that fits loosely enough to allow a comfortable stance, swing, and follow-through.

These Boots Are Made for Walkin'

Golf is predominantly a walking game. Despite the fact that courses make so much money by renting power carts, golf requires a lot of walking. So make sure you wear comfortable golf shoes. You will enjoy the experience a lot more if you are not torturing your feet all day long.

And while you're at it, make sure those comfortable golf shoes have the soft plastic spikes that are required by virtually all golf courses these days. The soft spikes are easy on the greens and better for your feet, legs, and back. But the real benefit of wearing spikes is that your feet won't slip when you are lunging and lurching at your shot.

Make Par While the Sun Shines

Appropriate golf attire will cover most of what needs to be covered at the golf course, but that still leaves a great deal uncovered. Whatever is left to the elements should also be covered, not with clothing, but with sunscreen. It's a toss-up as to whether this topic should be considered as part of the clothing discussion or the safety discussion. But it so important that it cannot be forgotten as you prepare for your round.

The Words and Wisdom on Golf

Isn' it fun to go out on the course and lie in the sun?

—Boo Hope

Golfers, especially those in warmer, sunnier climates spend a great deal of time absorbing the damaging rays of the sun. If people were designed to spend that much time in the sun they would come equipped with long shaggy coats of fur, but that wouldn't be nearly as interesting around the pool—no offense to the *Golfing Gorilla*.

Keeping Up With the Bobby Joneses

Wear clothes that are comfortable, but dignified.

Men: slacks, shorts, shirts with collars; no jeans, cut-offs, tank tops.

Women: slacks, shorts, skirts; no jeans, cut-offs.

Comfy golf shoes with soft spikes are recommended.

Have plenty of sunscreen for every golfer, every time you play.

No matter what your complexion, several hours in the bright sunshine requires a healthy lathering up with some good quality sunscreen. An SPF level of at least 15 is recommended (but 35 is probably more like it) for golfers, whose passion keeps them in the sun for several hours at a time. And for those who don't have as much covering on top, a hat (not a visor) is strongly recommended.

Is That a Sleeve of Golf Balls in Your Pocket ...

Or are you just happy to be playing golf? When one looks at the amazing array of equipment that is available to the average golfer, it is easy to be truly impressed by the ingenuity of the marketing mind, the vast complexity of the market itself, and the insatiable appetite of the golf consumer. One is also reminded of the immortal words of P. T. Barnum: "A sucker is born every minute."

You'll no doubt have lots of crucial junk that you've managed to shove into your golf bag, but let's pass on all of the stupid stuff a golfer can buy to help figure out how to swing the club. Instead, let's focus on the few things you need to have in your pocket or near at hand during your round:

- A couple of tees
- An extra golf ball
- A ball marker for on the green (a coin or medallion will do fine)
- A ball mark repair tool (two-pronged tool for fixing marks on the green)

One repair tool is usually sufficient, but I always carry two ball markers since there are many times when I find it convenient to mark someone else's ball to save time and help maintain a good *pace of play*. (Of course, you wouldn't do that in a tournament or competitive round, but in a friendly round, it's no problem.)

Playing With a Handicap

If you plan to play golf on anything that resembles a regular basis, it is a good idea to participate in the *handicap* system sponsored by the *USGA*. According to the USGA, "the purpose of the USGA Handicap System is to make the game of golf more enjoyable by enabling players of differing abilities to compete on an equitable basis."

Based on the scores posted, the system calculates a rating for each golfer. Then through a very simple set of calculations that anyone with a Ph.D. in Nuclear Physics and a Ouija board can understand, you can get strokes from someone who is better than you. It would certainly test the limits of something called a *Pocket Idiot's Guide* to fully fathom all the intricacies of the handicap system, but take my word for it, a handicap is a good thing to have.

First and foremost, maintaining a handicap will enable you to clearly monitor your improvement. As the season progresses and you see your index number coming down, you will know that all of the practice and hard work is paying off. Of course, there is a flip side to this point, but we needn't go there.

And a handicap is often required if you want to participate in club, corporate, or charity events. One of the great joys of playing golf is participating in the wide variety of charity golf events that are sponsored each year by so many worthy causes. You can participate as an individual or as a corporate sponsor and feel wonderful about doing something of value for your fellow human beings while playing the game you love. And in order to do so, you need a handicap.

Keeping Up With the Bobby Joneses

Register with a club or association that sponsors USGA handicaps.

You can monitor progress and see your potential as a golfer.

Don't try the USGA's math at home—take their word for it.

Tee for Two, or Four

I suppose it's possible to just show up at a golf course and announce your foursome's intention to play a round of golf, and be greeted with something other than a dumb stare or a sarcastic laugh. But it's not that likely. It's a much better idea to call ahead and make what is known in the golf world as a *tee time*.

Once you have set a tee time, it important to show up on time. One half hour before your appointed time is recommended. The advantage of having a tee time established and showing up on time is that you can prepare in a relaxed manner, hit a few balls, and practice a couple of putts before you go out and play. That helps you mentally prepare and sets the tone for a successful day.

Did You Know That?

Many courses now allow golfers to arrange their tee times via the Internet. In fact, some courses offer discounts for tee times made online. But even if that is not an option, the online connection does offer the advantage of 24-hour availability in arranging for your round of golf.

If you have scheduled a round of golf and you know ahead of time that you cannot play, it is the utmost of courtesy to call and cancel. There may be other groups calling who would love to be slipped right into your abandoned time slot. But if the golf course is still expecting you to show up, they will lose out on that revenue. And believe it or not, golf courses need the greens fees to survive.

If you are a single and want to play, then it is quite customary to show up and get put on the list of other singles waiting to play. You can putt or chip while you wait to get teamed up with a group who needs a fourth. Joining a group can be a great way to meet new people who share your passion for the game, but be sure that your knowledge and execution of golf rules and etiquette are "up to par" if you hope to keep those friends long.

The Least You Need to Know

- Safety is Rule #1 on the golf course. To avoid injuries, look all around before you take any practice swings, and be careful not to walk into someone else's practice swing.

- Be sure that the group ahead of you is well out of range before you hit your shot in their direction. This action should never be taken to urge a group to speed up their play. If you hit a shot that has any chance of striking another player, give plenty of warning by hollering, "Fore!"

- If thunderstorms appear to be forming around the golf course, use caution and head quickly to the clubhouse for protection. Consult the GCSAA suggestions on how to avoid getting struck by lightning.

- Maintain a positive attitude on the golf course to ensure that you (and everyone around you) enjoy the day and play your best.

- Register to maintain a USGA handicap so you can see your progress in the game and so you can fully participate in corporate and charity golf events.

- Set up a tee time in advance to be sure you and your group will be able to play; and cancel that tee time with plenty of notice if you are unable to play as scheduled.

Chapter

General Etiquette

In This Chapter

- Quiet on the set
- Practice makes perfect … or not
- Hitchin' a ride
- Lay your burden down—take a caddy
- Maintain the current course

The first time I walked out onto a golf course I was a fourteen-year-old caddy. And I soon sensed there was something unusual about this game of golf. It was different than any other game I had ever seen or played.

Clearly, some things were the same as other games. The participants played with an obvious passion, they wanted to play their best and were very disappointed when they didn't—and I mean *very* disappointed. But even though they sincerely wanted to win, they went out of their way to provide every advantage to the very people they were trying to beat! How could you *not* fall in love with a game that great?

I learned the voluntary behaviors I was seeing were part of a centuries-old tradition called "golf etiquette." There are no real rules of etiquette; there are no sanctions or penalties if you don't extend these courtesies. But every golfer seemed to know and understand that golf etiquette makes the game better for everyone.

And here is the best part about golf etiquette: everyone can do it. Not every golfer can hit the ball three hundred yards right down the middle (some can't hit it three hundred feet right down the middle). But every golfer can respect the course, respect the golfers around them, and respect the traditions of the game. If you accomplish nothing else as a golfer, become an expert at golf etiquette—the game will be better for your efforts.

All Quiet on the Western Front Nine

Golf is different than most other games in that it happens in relative silence. Why is it that a baseball player can hit a 90-mile-per-hour fastball in front of a roaring crowd, but a golfer needs complete silence? As famed golf-author P. G. Wodehouse wrote, a golfer can be distracted by the annoying "sound of a butterfly's wings flapping in a distant meadow."

The difference is this: hitting a 90-mile-an-hour fastball requires keen reflexes, instinct, and quick reaction time. There is really no time to think about the ball; you simply react to the ball. In golf, the ball is not moving (if it does move, you incur a *penalty stroke*). The golfer initiates the action; therefore the golfer has plenty of time to think about anything and everything.

Did You Know That?

You should remain quiet on the golf course when others are hitting or preparing to hit (tees, fairways, greens), when your foursome is near another group who is hitting, and when you are on the practice green or range before your round.

The essence of golf etiquette is to voluntarily extend the courtesies others need in order to fully succeed. Whether you are on the tee, in the fairway, on the green, or even on the practice green, always maintain a quiet demeanor and your friends will certainly appreciate your courtesy.

Don't Just Do Something ... Stand There!

Closely related to the practice of remaining quiet when another golfer is hitting, is the equally important practice of standing in a place that will be unobtrusive. When a golfer is preparing to hit, whether that is on the tee, in the fairway, or on the green, the other golfers in the group should cease all activity.

"Where is the best place to stand?" you ask. Let's use a clock analogy and say that when the golfer is at the address position, there is a straight line running through the golf ball down the target line. Let's also say the target position (e.g., the fairway or green) is at the 12:00 position on the clock. (Just in case you're wondering, that is 12:00 P.M., since if it were 12:00 A.M. you wouldn't be able to see the target very well.)

Now, with a right-handed golfer addressing the ball at the 9:00 position, the remaining golfers should stand somewhere between 3:00 and 4:00, preferably around 3:35 (which would be across from the golfer and a bit to the right). No one should ever stand at or near the 6:00 position since that would put you right in the peripheral vision of the golfer and even the slightest movement there would be detected and very distracting.

Note that this information mainly relates to positions on the tee because in the fairway and on the green the group will be more spread out and getting ready for their own shots.

Standing still in exactly the right spot is the ideal for which we all strive. However, reality dictates that many times, especially when playing ready golf, you will be caught in a spot that is not perfect just as someone is getting ready to hit. When that happens, as it inevitably will, just stop what you are doing, stand still and wait until the golfer has completed the swing. Stop fumbling through your golf bag, stop all the practice swings and by all means, stop all conversation.

And remember that you are standing still to avoid creating distractions, but are also in a perfect position to watch where the shot goes. By paying attention and marking where the ball lands, you may save your group precious time that would otherwise be spent looking for a lost ball.

Take a Message!

The use of cell phones has become a divisive issue as it pertains to driving cars, attending movies, eating in restaurants, and working in the office. There are even people who have had the audacity to use their cell phones at funerals. And worse than that, there are people who use their cell phones on the golf course.

The Words and Wisdom on Golf

There's no game like golf: you go out with three friends, play eighteen holes, and return with three enemies.

—Anonymous

Cell phones ring at unpredictable times and people speak too loudly when they are on their cell phones. Plus it is very awkward to hit a perfect little chip shot close to the pin when you have your cell phone tucked under your chin. So decide to turn your cell phone off and leave it in your bag during your round of golf. Everyone in your foursome will be grateful.

Proper Shadow Management

Closely tied to the notion of remaining quiet on the golf course is the idea of keeping your shadow out of view of the golfer who is hitting. Nothing is more distracting when you are deep in concentration on the shot you're about to flub than to have someone's shadow fleetingly flit across your line of vision.

The Words and Wisdom on Golf

These greens are so fast I have to hold my putter over the ball and hit it with the shadow.

—Sam Snead

You should never let your shadow cast across a ball, the line of a putt, the hole, or anything related to the shot that is about to happen. Even if a golfer is just lining up a shot, be careful not to cause a distraction with your shadow.

Keeping Up With the Bobby Joneses

On tee, fairway, green, and practice green, respectfully maintain quiet.

Remember that golfers in the groups around you need quiet, too.

Stand in a place that will create the least interference for the golfer who is hitting.

Keep your shadow away from the line of vision of golfers who are hitting.

Golf Etiquette Begins at the Range

Golf is a game that requires a lot of practice. Personally I have given up on the idea of practicing so I can get better: I now practice all the time just to keep from getting worse. But whether you practice to improve, or to maintain your skills, you will find yourself spending lots of time at the practice range.

There are several different aspects to the game and each requires a different set of skills, therefore each demands its own specific attention and practice regimen.

Did You Know That?

According to the National Golf Foundation, in 2005 36.2 million Americans, ages 5 years old or over, either played a regulation round of golf or visited a practice facility. And 26.2 million Americans, ages 18 or over, played at least one regulation round of golf.

But since we are focused on rules and etiquette, and not on the practical application of the swing, let's discuss the etiquette issues at the range.

Good golf etiquette begins at the range. It is here that you can hone the skills required to be an excellent golfer, not only in how you hit the ball, but in how you respect the rights of others to practice and play as well.

There are some common themes that you will see throughout the game that clearly translate to your time on the range.

- Safety—Stay behind the safety line when walking at the range; stay in your own box when swinging a club; hit one ball at a time; never aim at the *ball picker*.

- Quiet—Practice quietly; if you are having difficulty, don't let your frustration bother the other golfers.

- Courtesy—Return your empty buckets to the dispenser.

- Children—Keep kids under control; no running or screaming.

- Family-Friendly—If you are not accustomed to using G-rated language, then use the range as an opportunity to learn that aspect of good golf etiquette.

Hold Your Fire!

Occasionally you will need to run out onto the range because a club has broken or slipped out of your hands. The safe approach is to go to the person running the range and have an announcement made to "hold your fire" for a moment so you can run out and retrieve your club.

Never run out onto the range to retrieve a club or pick up extra balls when other golfers are hitting.

Lessons—Take Them; Don't Give Them

People go to the range to try to find their swing, but the golf swing is rarely easy to find. That is why when you cruise up and down the length of a practice range you will see a wide variety of swing styles, none of which closely resemble that of, say, Tiger Woods. Or even Tiger Woods as a 6-year-old.

The Words and Wisdom on Golf

It's a funny thing, the more I practice the luckier I get.

—Attributed to Arnold Palmer, Ben Hogan, and Lee Trevino

It is difficult to see people in pain (or at least painful to watch what they are doing). So after you hit two good shots in a row, there is a tendency to believe you have mastered the game. So you might feel inclined to reach out to your fellow human to try to ease her burden with your expert analysis on all the things she is doing wrong.

Nine times out of ten your generosity will not be rewarded. The rule of thumb here should be, "Mind your own business." When you get your PGA card, then you can hang out a shingle and start to give lessons and share all the wisdom you have accumulated. Till then, that kind of advice is more of a bother than any degree of help.

The Practice Green

The practice green is a very important part of your preparation for the day ahead. But if the practice green is crowded, there are a few considerations that will make your experience more useful to you as a golfer and remove any likelihood of confrontations:

- Limit yourself to two or three golf balls at the practice green.
- Limit yourself to short practice putts (under 10 feet).
- Don't block holes to which others are putting.
- Respectful quiet is always appreciated.

Keeping Up With the Bobby Joneses

Safety: watch for swinging clubs and only swing your clubs while you are in a designated box.

Quiet: no idle chit-chat, no cells phones, no nonsense. Don't give lessons.

Don't wander out onto the range; if you need to retrieve a club, have an announcement made.

Use only a couple of golf balls to practice putting.

If there are others around, only practice short putts.

Don't set up near a hole someone else might be using.

On the practice green you should be focusing on your stroke. Keep it smooth, and keep it straight. This is not the time to practice those 50-foot double benders that snake their way through 12 other golfers trying to work out their *yips*. Practice those at a time when you have the place all to yourself.

Golf Carts: The Path to Glory

As mentioned earlier, golf is predominantly a walking game. Six hundred years ago on the linksland of Scotland where the game originated, the humble shepherds who devised the game did not tool about in little motorized carts.

Somewhere between the late 1400s and now (it was actually around the mid-1950s) golf carts came into prominence and have had a major impact on the development of the game, particularly on the design of golf courses. Many courses today are specifically laid out with carts in mind to take players on the long-distance journey between the green and the next tee.

The Words and Wisdom on Golf

Many a golfer prefers a golf cart to a caddy because the cart cannot count, criticize, or laugh.

—Anonymous

With carts as a regular part of the game, it is important to understand the rules of etiquette that apply. There are three options for cart rules that might be in effect when you play, so it is important to make a note of which conditions apply and obey those regulations for the day.

The three cart options you may encounter are:

- No Restrictions—means you can drive the cart "anywhere." But, really, on a day when there are no cart restrictions it still means only drive in the fairway or rough, on the cart path, and directly to the snack shop *at the turn*. Never drive a cart onto a teeing area, near the greens, into *bunkers*, or areas designated as *hazards* or *OB*.

- 90-Degree Rule—means you should drive the cart on the path up to the point at which you are even with your golf ball. Then turn 90 degrees and drive straight to your ball; return straight to the path after you have hit your shot. Proceed up the cart path to where that shot now lies and do it again.

- Cart Path Only—means you must keep the cart on the path throughout your round. This rule is generally reserved for a time when the fairways are in particularly sloppy conditions and the carts could do severe damage to the turf.

The "cart path only" rule often requires a little planning when your ball lies across the fairway from the cart path because you won't be able to drive your clubs right up to where your shot is located.

To operate most efficiently under the cart path only rule:

- Observe your lie as you drive up the cart path.
- Plan your shot based on yardage markers or other distance indicators.
- Take a few extra clubs that will provide you with other alternatives in case Plan A doesn't work out.
- Remember to pick up all of your clubs before you head back to the cart.

Whether you are using a motorized golf cart or a pull cart, it is important to think about where you park it when someone else is hitting. Obviously, while teeing off, the cart will be parked on the cart path well away from the tee boxes, but what about while you're in the fairway?

Just be sure of two things: first, that you have given the golfer plenty of room to swing freely without worry that he will be in danger of hitting something or someone with the swing; and second, that you are well out of the peripheral vision of the golfer hitting.

You should park the cart so that it is not on the line of shot he is intending to hit, but instead you should ideally be 90 degrees off that line and well behind the golfer.

As you get close to the green, you will generally see signs guiding the carts away from the green, off the fairway, and back over onto the cart path. Follow those and all other directions for carts and you will have a wonderful round. Well, at least you won't get lost.

Keeping Up With the Bobby Joneses

Safety First: drive at safe speeds, always under control.

Keep carts away from tees, greens, and restricted areas.

Determine cart rules for the day.

No Restrictions: ride in fairways, rough, and path only; not in hazards, bunkers, or OB.

90-Degree Rule: stay on path until even with ball; turn 90 degrees, ride out to ball, and return to path after hitting.

Cart Path Only: stay on path; bring extra clubs when you walk to your ball to hit.

Don't park too close to a golfer who is hitting; leave plenty of room for swinging.

Follow signs directing traffic on and off path.

Who's on Your Bag?

There is no greater treat in golf than playing a fine golf course with the assistance of a knowledgeable caddy. You can experience the thrill of walking the course unencumbered by your clubs and focusing completely on the next shot you will take. Your caddy is on your team. He is there to help assess your shots, to celebrate the success of a great shot, and to grieve with you over a bad shot (for an extra tip, he'll even take the blame for the bad shot).

Caddying (or looping, as it is called) used to provide many young people with an excellent opportunity to make some money and learn the great game of golf right up close. Unfortunately there are far fewer courses that offer caddy services these days, so you often have to go to the more elite courses to have that experience.

The Words and Wisdom on Golf

The term caddy is derived from the French word, *cadet*. It means a young soldier.

But if it is not a regular part of your game, you owe it to yourself to give it a try. There are a few points to note in terms of etiquette when utilizing the assistance of a caddy.

There's an old joke among caddies that they live by the rules of Ups: show up, keep up, shut up. But really, an experienced caddy knows the course very well and may only take a few holes or a few shots to assess your game. From then on, he will be able to advise you on distances and club selection. Respect your caddy as an asset to your game and seriously consider any advice given.

> ### The Words and Wisdom on Golf
>
> Golfer: Caddy, do you think I can get there with my five-iron?
> Caddy: Eventually

Tipping a caddy is a question that is often posed on the Mr. Golf Etiquette website. Not whether you should tip a caddy, but how much you should tip a caddy. I consulted with the director of the caddy program at Bandon Dunes, in Oregon, one of the finest golf facilities in the country and a golf course that fully embraces the idea of the caddy as an integral part of the game.

> ### Keeping Up With the Bobby Joneses
>
> Enjoy the unique experience of playing golf with the services of a caddy.
>
> Make the caddy a part of your team and benefit from her expertise regarding the course.
>
> Be generous in tipping your caddy if he provided you a great service and made it a special day.

He suggested that if the player is satisfied with the performance of the caddy, the tip should be one half of the base fee for the caddy's service (e.g., a $25 tip for a $50 fee). He also commented that if the caddy has done an outstanding job for the golfer and really helped to make it a special day, a tip equal to the fee is probably appropriate.

One hundred dollars may seem like a lot to pay for a caddy, but think about this: years from now, looking back on that round of golf, you won't think about the money, but you'll have some wonderful memories from that magical day of golf.

Care and Feeding of the Golf Course

Golf courses are generally places of pristine beauty. A remarkable amount of work has gone into designing and constructing the course, and a heroic effort is made by the grounds crew to maintain it in its original condition. But after all that, it would still be impossible to keep a golf course at peak playing condition if golfers did not take responsibility for fixing what they had disturbed.

In addition, golfers operate under a rule of golf (that will be discussed in detail in Chapter 3) known as play it as it lies. If golfers are required to play the ball as it lies, then a supreme effort is required to ensure that the ball does not lie in trouble that could easily have been avoided. And that means that all golfers are relying on the courtesy and etiquette of their fellow golfers to clean up after themselves.

Divots

The ball leaves the face of your club, and instantly upon contact you know the shot is right. There is a purity about the well-hit shot that is unmistakable. Ben Hogan called that feeling the "greatest pleasure" in golf. And you watch that shot rise and streak toward the target and you appreciate the fact that, yes, life is good.

The Words and Wisdom on Golf

What other people may find in poetry or art museums, I find in the flight of a good drive.

—Arnold Palmer

Then, as you approach the ball and ready yourself for the payoff shot, right up at the flag, you look down in horror! You have done everything you were supposed to do, the ball has done everything it was supposed to do, but somebody did not do something very important that they were supposed to do. And the ball has landed in an unfilled divot hole. I hate when that happens!

That haunting rule of golf strikes again: *play it as it lies.* Just because your ball landed in a divot that someone else neglected to fix does not mean that you get to move your ball. Instead it means you have the decided disadvantage of hitting it out of that hole and risking disaster as you take your next shot.

There are two methods that are generally available to you to take care of this modest greens-keeping task, and they are as follows:

- Replace the divot—Retrieve the piece of turf that was dislodged by the shot and replace it into the hole left by the shot. Step down on it gently to secure it in place and move on.
- Fill the Divot—In most instances, if you are riding, the carts will include a container of sand and seed mixture that simply needs to be sprinkled into the hole.

If you take the seconds required to repair the divots you create, the turf will have a far greater chance to regenerate than if you leave them empty. The golfers behind you will never know who you are or what you did, because your effort will be covered over with beautiful new grass. But they will all thank you in their own way—by filling in the divots that they create.

A Day at the Beach

No one plans to hit a ball into the sand. It's always a big disappointment when it happens, especially compared to the many other places you could have hit it, like the fairway or the green. But like the saying goes, golf is a lot like life. And in this case it means the reason you're in trouble is because you did it to yourself.

Regardless of how you got in, you now have to get out. But before you step into that bunker, there are a few rules of golf and points of etiquette that you need to know to avoid taking on any penalty strokes or losing any friends.

The following are rules to observe when in a bunker:

- Don't ground your club in the bunker (that means don't touch the ground—not even during your back swing [two-stroke penalty]).

- Don't test the sand to see how hard or soft it is—not with your club, hands, or feet; you may shift your feet as you secure your stance, but you may not kick the sand around to see how firm it is.

- Don't "build" a stance in the sand; if your ball is on an uphill lie, or up the face of a bunker, don't bring a bunch of sand together to improve your stance; take your lie as you find it.

The following etiquette should be observed when in a bunker:

- Enter the bunker from the low side; if it is a steep-faced bunker, walk around to the low side, but don't climb up or down the face of the bunker.

- After you hit out of the bunker rake away any traces of where the ball landed, your footprints, and your stroke; leave the bunker in a smooth condition so no golfer will later end up in your footprints or *sand divot*.

A burning question lingers in the minds of golfers everywhere. I can hear you all asking it right now. Where should I leave the rake, in the bunker or out? Some golfers advocate leaving rakes in because they believe nothing should prevent the ball from going into a bunker if it was on course to do that. Others think the rakes should be outside because if the ball does enter the trap, then nothing should prevent it from rolling to its natural resting place. Both are good points.

Here is the bottom line: the rakes should be left outside the bunkers with the handles running parallel to the fairway. That way the rakes will be least likely to impact a ball headed for the bunker, but nothing will impede the ball once it is inside.

Since there is a wide range of opinions on the topic, here is a reasonable approach to take: when you play golf, look around to see where the rakes are positioned at that course. Then simply follow the policy of that course for the day. When in Rome ....

The Least You Need to Know

- Maintain a respectful quiet demeanor whenever someone is hitting; quiet should be observed for people in groups other than your own, too. Turn your cell phone off before you begin to play.

- Be sure your shadow is not cast onto the ball or ball path that someone is hitting; keep your shadow off the hole and out of the peripheral vision of anyone hitting.

- At the practice range observe the rules of safety and quiet; don't give unsolicited advice; closely supervise children; and use the experience at the range to teach children good golf etiquette.

- If the practice green is crowded, limit yourself to short putts and a couple of balls; don't block holes that others are using; and keep your feet away from holes.

- Drive carts at safe speeds; keep carts off tees and greens; and observe posted rules such as *90-degree rule* and *cart path only*. If cart path only, then take extra clubs to your ball just in case.

- Be courteous when asking to *play through* another group, or if your group is being played through. Replace your divots, and rake your bunkers.

Chapter 3

Play It as It Lies

In This Chapter

- You have the honors
- At the launching pad
- Every lie needs a little improving
- Can you give me a lift?
- Making every shot count—once each

Okay golfers, you have now reached the moment of truth. You've dressed up, lathered up, and showed up and now you're ready to play some golf. But before you do, let's review one very important item, and that is: exactly how the heck do you play this game, anyway?

Let's face it: the concept of golf is quite simple. You hit the ball and it goes into a little hole; repeat seventeen times and head to the clubhouse for a cold one. But just to make it a little more interesting, a couple of rules and protocols have evolved over the last six hundred years that you might want to consider. So in this chapter we'll start to take a look at how the game is actually played. That way, when you get out there you can feel smart and look good—until you swing the club, that is.

Who's Turn Is It Anyway?

The *order of play* in golf is generally simple: the one who is farthest from the hole hits next. But there are a couple of situations that require a little extra discussion.

The rule that dictates order of play is short and sweet and is pretty easy to fathom, which makes it unique among golf rules. Boiled down to its essence, it tells you how to decide who goes first at the beginning of the round, who goes first on subsequent tees, and who goes in what order through the play of a hole.

Getting Teed Off

At the first tee, before the round begins, order of play is decided by a type of lottery. What most golfers do is arrange their foursome in a rough circle and toss a tee into the air. If it lands facing you, you go first; do that again two more times to determine second and third, and the remaining player goes last.

On subsequent tees throughout the round, the player or team with the lowest score on the previous hole gets the *honor*. That is, the player with honors has the privilege of hitting first on the next tee. If there is a tie on a given hole, then the one with the best score on the previous hole retains the honors until someone else wins the privilege away.

Beyond the Tees

Other than on the tees, the order of play is determined by who is farthest from the hole. Once you have all hit your tee shots and gone to your respective balls, it can then be determined who hits next. It does not matter whose ball lies what number of strokes; the only concern is the distance to the hole.

Did You Know That?

Golfers can agree to play out of turn for reasons of convenience; for instance, golfer number one may be away, but if he hits he will step too near the ball of golfer number two, so he lets golfer number two hit first. But golfers may not play out of turn for purposes of one gaining an advantage, for instance, seeing how a ball will roll. In a tournament, that can lead to disqualification.

Allowing the farthest player out to hit, if not the exact intention of the rule, ensures that the group stays together throughout the round. If the players who hit farthest could hit whenever they were ready, it would be likely they would end up way ahead of the shorter hitters and the group would be spread all over the place. It would also put the longer hitters up in front of the shorter hitters and, as we discussed in Chapter 1, that would be dangerous.

On the Dance Floor

When the game of golf first evolved, there was no discernable difference between the green and the fairway as there is today. The game was played over some pretty rough pasture to a simple hole in the ground. And the rule regarding order of play was one of the first to develop.

Order of play on the green is the same as elsewhere on the course: the one who is farthest away plays first.

A situation that occasionally creates confusion regarding order of play occurs when the players are approaching the green. Some players might be on the green and some off, and it becomes unclear as to whether the group should wait until everyone is on the green before the group begins to putt. It seems like a reasonable courtesy to wait until everyone hits onto the green, and it does make *tending the flag* easier.

However, the distinction between being on or off the green is an artificial one. The rule regarding order of play is clear. Therefore, if someone is off the green, and 20 feet away from the hole, and someone else is on the green but 60 feet away, who goes first? The answer is always the same: the one who is farthest away.

Playing From the Teeing Ground

There is an official place called the *teeing ground*. It is the area between the markers that you see on the tees, and it also extends backward two club lengths from the front edge of those markers. The grounds crew will move those markers every day to make sure that the wear and tear created by shoes and clubs gets evenly distributed around the tees. Moving them also creates an interesting variety of shots for the golfers.

Did You Know That?

If you accidentally bump the ball with your club while you are getting ready to tee off, and the ball falls off the tee, guess what? No penalty! That's because when your ball is on the tee it is not yet in play. If you move the ball while getting ready to hit elsewhere on the course, a penalty stroke is incurred and you must replace the ball.

Golfers are allowed to choose a spot anywhere within the teeing ground from which to tee off. Most people try to get right up front, but it is most important to find an area where your stance is level. And remember that even though the ball has to be in the teeing ground, you can stand outside the teeing ground. But you are not allowed to move those markers in order to accommodate your stance or to find a more level spot.

Etiquette on the Tee

Every golf course offers a variety of tee boxes so golfers can choose the length that is appropriate for their abilities. Typically there is a red tee up front, a white tee in the middle, and a blue tee at the back, but there can be quite a bit of variety on this theme. Some courses provide five levels of tees, including championship tees way in the back for tournament play.

The first step to good golf etiquette on the tee is to choose the tees that match your game. Many people, particularly those of the male persuasion, have a tendency to overestimate their ability to hit the long ball so they choose to play *from the tips*. Of course, when they get out onto the course they are quickly reminded of the reason they have day jobs such as accountant and salesman.

Higher-handicap golfers who play too far back tend to swing harder to make up the distance, and that usually leads to problems in their game. In an effort to discourage people from playing a length that may exceed their abilities, some courses require a handicap of 10 or better to play the blue or back tees. There is no stigma associated with playing the course at 6,300 yards or so, which is a typical distance for white tees. And there are several benefits.

When you play the course at the proper length:

- You play quicker
- You lose fewer golf balls

- You hit more greens on the par 3s
- You score better
- You have more fun

By the way, that last item in the list is a direct result of all the other items. So play the course at a length that works best for your game.

General Housekeeping on the Tee

When your group is teeing off, stand in a place that is as unobtrusive as possible. Do not position yourself such that you are looking down the line of the shot (that is, at the 6 o'clock position to a right-handed golfer). Any movement on your part could be picked up in the peripheral vision of the golfer and would be very distracting.

Motorized carts should be left at the path, as noted earlier, but pull carts and carry bags should also be positioned somewhere off the tee box. When you are leaving the tee, do not pull your handcarts across tee boxes. Even if you think the wheels will not make marks in the surface of the tees, your effort to keep your cart off the tee will demonstrate that you are a person who cares about the game and maintaining the course.

When every golfer in your group has hit, including any *provisional balls* that may be necessary, be ready to move out. Whether you are walking or riding, carrying or pulling, provide a good example by keeping the game moving forward at a healthy pace.

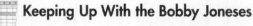

Keeping Up With the Bobby Joneses

Play from the tees that are right for the length of your game.

Stand in a place where you will not bother the person teeing off.

Leave golf carts and carry bags off to the side of the teeing area; do not pull carts across the tee boxes.

Watch the tee shots from all players to help in finding those balls.

Be ready to move out promptly when everyone in your group has hit.

Improving Your Lie

Probably the most basic and well-known rule of golf is, "play it as it lies." That rule embodies so much of the essence of the game of golf as it first evolved. Golf is quite often a test of character as much as a test of skill. It presents the golfer with bad bounces, bad lies, bad luck, bad breaks, and bad stuff of all kinds. But "play it as it lies" tells the golfer to "deal with it."

And that's not unfair; that's the way it should be. The game was born in the great outdoors on rough, seaside terrain carved out by wind and weather. It wouldn't be a challenging game if you could just put the ball wherever you wanted if the lie didn't suit your liking, or if it was too hard for you. That would be a game for weenies.

Let's find out what happens in some of the important aspects of playing your ball as it lies—and stop that sniveling!

Lie, Stance, Swing, and Line

The rules of golf only prohibit improving four things: your lie, stance, swing, and line. Okay, so ... lie, stance, swing, and line; what else is there that you can improve? Well, you can always improve the company you keep, but that's covered in a different *Idiot's Guide*.

Lie. Improving your lie does not include telling better fibs about the shots you took on the last hole. It does, however, include pressing down behind the ball with your foot in order to create a better possibility of connecting with the ball. Anything that alters or improves the natural lie of the ball violates the letter and spirit of this rule; when in doubt, play it as it lies.

The Words and Wisdom on Golf

The difference in golf and government is that in golf you can't improve your lie.
—George Deukmejian

Believe it or not, improving your lie would even include shaking the water off the branch of a tree before you get under the tree to hit your shot and wiping the morning dew off the grass behind your ball before you hit. One could probably safely assume it would include removing the molten lava from around your ball if you were playing in Hawaii during an eruption.

Stance. A player is entitled to take a fair stance when addressing the ball, but may not *build a stance*. That seems easy enough to understand, but, then again, this is a rule of golf, so don't be too hasty.

What if you were hitting out of a very wet area and you threw down a piece of wood so you could keep your shoes dry? Busted!

Did You Know That?

In 1987, while playing in a PGA event, Craig Stadler hit a ball that landed under a tree. He placed a towel on the ground so he could kneel down to take his next shot without getting mud on his pants. That action was deemed to be building a stance. Incidentally, the rule violation was spotted by a TV viewer who called in; and because Stadler had already finished the round and signed his card with an incorrect score, he was disqualified from the tournament.

What if your ball is up in a tree and you stand on your power cart to hit your ball into the fairway? That, too, qualifies as building a stance. Consider this: if you put your foot on a boulder that was there as a natural part of the course, that would be fine, but if you rolled that boulder from somewhere else just so you could stand on it or put your foot on it, that would violate the rule.

So you see, building a stance can take on a variety of forms that you might not expect. Be careful; it's a penalty jungle out there.

Swing. The *area of intended swing* is one of those things that amateur golfers deal with all the time—mainly because they play a lot of their golf in places other than the fairway. If you are often in the trees and bushes and brambles, you will know about the kind of things that can affect the area of your intended swing.

The prohibition on improving the area of your intended swing prevents golfers from breaking branches, taking down fences, knocking down old barns, and plucking the leaves off dandelions. It enables you to take your swing, but not if you have to alter the course in order to do it.

In essence you are not allowed to move, bend, or break anything growing or fixed (nor "fold, spindle, and mutilate"). If you do any of those things in preparation for your swing, you are in violation of the rules.

Line of Play. The *line of play* is the direction that the player wishes the ball to take after the stroke. It also incorporates a little bit to each side of that line and the vertical space above it. And in some ways it would seem difficult to have an impact on that line, but on the contrary, it turns out to be quite easy.

Let's say you are hitting out from under some trees, but one little branch is hanging down and obscuring the path you have chosen. So you take that branch and hook it over the top of a bigger one just above it. You have not broken anything and you have caused no damage to the course. But you have improved the line of play and therefore you are the proud new owner of a two-stroke penalty. Congratulations and thanks for playing—next time play by the rules!

The line-of-play rule is often applicable during play on the green where the line of play is very clearly right along the ground between your ball and the hole. So here are some things to be careful for regarding line of play on the green:

- Your ball lies on the apron between the green and a bunker; your opponent hits out of the sand and covers the area around your ball with sand; you get to clean that up with no penalty (you are entitled to the lie your stroke gave you).

- Your fellow competitor or opponent improves his line of play by repairing spike marks on the green and your line is improved as a result of that action and you approve that action, even by simply not objecting to it, you get a penalty along with him.

- You are playing golf on a frosty autumn morning and you have a 4-footer for birdie. You are very anxious to sink this since you just got a triple on the last hole. So you lightly brush aside the frosty morning dew on the path from your ball to the hole—and, just like that, you are now putting for bogey because of the two-stroke penalty you incurred.

See how fun this is?

Keep in mind that there are many exceptions through which the golfer is allowed *free relief*, and several of those situations will be covered in Chapter 6. Meanwhile, approach every shot with the most basic of all golf rules in the forefront of your mind: play it as it lies.

Local Rules

A facet of playing the ball as it lies that can vary from course to course is the impact that particular, peculiar, or problematic features of the golf course may present to the golfer. Though always under the approval and sanction of the USGA, the golf course may augment or adapt the rules to allow for their unique circumstances. These rules that only apply to a certain locality are very cleverly called *local rules*.

Local rules may take into consideration things like the high-tension wires that cross the ninth fairway (drive hits the wires, re-hit without penalty) or the flowerbeds behind the fourth green (*nearest point of relief*, not closer to the hole, without penalty).

The best place to educate yourself regarding local rules is on the back of the scorecard. The local rules are generally printed there and can save you strokes if you are aware of their existence. It is especially important to do if you are playing a course for the first time.

Environmentally Sensitive Areas

Many courses enhance the beauty of their layout by incorporating wetlands or other environmentally sensitive areas that are home to protected species of birds, coyotes, and other animals. Those areas are marked with special stakes (often red or yellow stakes with green tops) indicating they are environmentally sensitive. If you hit into that area, you may not enter to look for your ball.

Instead you must play according to the rule associated with the stake or marking for the area, taking any penalty strokes as indicated (covered in Chapter 5 and on the tear-out card). For instance, if the environmentally sensitive area is designated by red stakes with green tops, you should play it as a standard red-staked area with one exception. In a standard red-staked area you would have the option to hit the ball without penalty, if you deemed it playable. But because you cannot go get that ball from the environmentally sensitive area, that option is not available to you.

The environment is very important to all of us; in fact, it is one of my favorite places to play when I am outdoors. So be respectful of those beautiful parts of the golf course. And if you don't want to lose that golf ball, don't hit it into the environment.

Lifting, Dropping, Placing

Despite the fundamental admonition within the rules of golf to play it as it lies, there are many instances throughout a round where you are allowed to, or in fact, *must* pick up a ball and do something with it besides simply playing it. And on the theory that everything that comes up must go down, once you have lifted a ball, it must either be dropped or placed somewhere. So let's see how that happens.

Lifting

The easiest "lift and drop" situation on the golf course is after you get the ball into the hole, you can lift it out and drop it into your pocket as you go to the next hole. The others are a little more involved, but still not too bad.

The first thing to remember before lifting a ball is that the ball is *in play*. So before it can be moved, it needs to be *marked*. And if it needs to be replaced somewhere (either by dropping or placing), then the marking is also instrumental in deciding exactly where the ball will be dropped or placed or where a measurement of one or two club lengths will begin.

The most common instance of lifting a ball is when marking and lifting your ball on the green. The mark lets you replace the ball at exactly the right spot.

Dropping

The technique for dropping is specified in the rules: stand erect, hold the ball at shoulder height and arm's length, and then drop.

The rules specify the location of the drop, e.g., within one club length of the point where the ball entered the hazard. And the rules always include a note that it must be dropped "no nearer the hole."

The Re-Drop

If you drop a ball and it lands in a place not allowed by the rules, then you must *re-drop* that ball. Here are some circumstances under which you must re-drop (without penalty):

- If the ball ends up in a hazard (assuming you did not start in the hazard)
- If the ball ends up outside a hazard (assuming you started inside the hazard)
- If the ball ends up on the putting green
- If the ball rolls out of bounds
- If the ball rolls back into the same situation you were dropping to get out of (except an unplayable lie)
- If the ball rolls more than two club lengths from where it hit the golf course when dropped
- If it ends up nearer the hole

If you re-drop and any of those items listed above happen again, you *must* then place the ball at the spot where the drop first hit the ground.

Placing and Replacing

Placing the ball is simple. As just noted, there is a spot designated by the rule, and you can simply put the ball there. (In the previous example, the ball is placed on the spot where your drop hit the golf course within one club length from the original spot of interference.)

Once a ball has been lifted and is being replaced, it must be replaced on the spot from which it was lifted. If you try to place or replace the ball on a designated spot and it won't stay there, you can move it to the nearest spot where it will stay, as long as it is not nearer the hole.

Did You Notice That Shot? The Whiff/Double Hit

A final thought in the area of playing the ball as it lies is to consider the definition of a golf swing.

The very essence of making a swing includes the intent to strike the ball and move it forward. So for instance, if you are lining up your tee shot and you accidentally bump the ball off the tee, that does not qualify as a swing or a stroke. There was no intent. Also, on the tee, the ball is not yet in play. But if you were in the fairway and accidentally moved your ball, you would incur a penalty stroke for moving a ball in play, and you must replace the ball before you hit again.

But what if you took a mighty wind up and thundering hack, but totally missed the ball (affectionately known as a *whiff*)? Does that count as a stroke? The answer lies in your intent. Since you intended to strike the ball and move it forward, but you simply missed, the result is that you do incur a stroke. This is also the case if your ball was on the tee.

The Words and Wisdom on Golf

Reverse every natural instinct and do the opposite of what you are inclined to do, and you will probably come very close to having a perfect golf swing.

—Ben Hogan

On the opposite end of the embarrassment spectrum from missing the ball altogether is hitting it more than once (the *double hit*). It happens more often than many people realize. As you're swinging, your club can get caught in some long grass that temporarily slows the club down. So you give the club a little extra oomph. Then, much to your shock and dismay, as Mr. Club comes tearing out of the long grass, it meets up with Mr. Ball, which was suspended in space by the wimpiness of the first contact made just moments ago.

The bad news is that the first contact counts as your stroke and any additional contact adds one penalty stroke, adding up to a total of two for that exercise.

The Least You Need to Know

- Toss a tee at the beginning to see who hits first (order of play); on the other tees use honors, or who scored best on the previous hole to see who hits first; elsewhere, order of play is determined by whoever is farthest from the hole.

- Don't improve your lie, build a stance, affect the line of your swing, or alter the line of play.

- Mark your ball before you lift it if it will be subsequently replaced or dropped back into play.

- The proper way to drop a ball is from shoulder height with arm outstretched, then simply drop straight down.

- A whiff, which is an intentional swing that unintentionally misses the ball, counts as one stroke.

- Making more than one contact with the ball with one swing, as in a double hit counts as two strokes.

Chapter 4

Pace of Play

In This Chapter

- Fire when ready
- Time savers on the tee
- Fairway faux pas
- Great green golf
- Mind if we play through?

Pace of play is one of the more controversial issues in the game of golf. It deals with the considerations related to the ever-lengthening time it takes to play a round of golf. Pace of play brings up an important question: if people love to play golf so much, why are they in such a big hurry to get off the golf course?

People who love golf are not "in a hurry to get off the course." They understand that golf is about rhythm and timing, and if they are standing around waiting for you to take 10 practice swings and *plumb-bob* your 3-inch putt, they lose their rhythm and timing.

From the late 1990s through the early 2000s, the number of people regularly playing golf declined.

One of the main reasons, cited by people who have given up the game, is very simple: slow play. A reasonable round of golf should take 4 to 4½ hours to play (in Ireland they consider 3 hours to be about right), but some courses around the United States are finding that rounds are averaging 5½ to 6 hours. That's *way* too long!

It is the responsibility of your group to stay within half a hole of the group ahead of you. If the group ahead is on the green when you are on the tee (on a par 4 or 5), then you are falling behind. If they are not in sight, then your group gets a very low grade in the pace-of-play department.

This chapter contains some very important tips to help you play your round of golf in a reasonable amount of time and make sure your golf report card includes straight As in pace of play.

Playing Ready Golf

In Chapter 3, we discussed the order of play dictated by the rules of golf. Those rules are required in any kind of tournament play. But in a casual round of golf it is often better to rely on *ready golf* to determine who hits next, especially on the tees.

Ready golf simply recognizes that, regardless of who scored best on the previous hole, one player might be ready before another. So the decision is made to allow the player who is ready to hit while the other is busy getting ready.

Here are some quick tips on playing ready golf:

- On the tee: it is generally clear who is ready, so let him or her hit; let the shorter hitters go first, to allow the group ahead to get safely out of range; if you have people hitting from different sets of tees, then allow the people farthest back to go first (also a safety precaution).

- In the fairway, where golf balls can be spread far and wide by the tee shots, it is not so easy to tell who is ready and who is preparing to hit now; be quite careful to look and see who is hitting and whether it is safe for you to hit before you proceed.

- On the green, it is a good idea to go back to the rule that the one who is farthest from the hole plays next. It will help avoid crossing ball paths and flag-tending issues.

Ready golf will save time and help your group to maintain its position behind the group ahead.

Of Tee I Sing!

When you are on the tee, there are several things you can do to help maintain a good pace and stay close to the group ahead of you.

- Choose the proper tees—the benefits of doing so are listed in Chapter 3.

- Watch where everyone's shot goes, and use a landmark to identify where the ball lands;

it will dramatically increase the likelihood of finding that ball and doing so quickly.

- If it seems likely your tee shot is lost, hit a provisional ball (don't search for the ball then determine it's lost and walk back to hit again); hit the provisional after everyone else has hit his or her first tee shot.

- Mark scores from the previous hole at the tee rather than on that green.

- Keep conversations to a minimum while people are hitting; carry on your conversations while you walk or ride to your ball.

Pace of play is not the same as rushing your game. It is about playing at a pace that enables you to stay focused and play your best.

Foiling Fairway Faux Pas Forever

When the game sends golfers in all directions after their tee shots, the pace of play can drag, so it is critical to stay in touch with what the others are doing and when the burden is on you to do something. Let's look at a few of the things that golfers need to know in order to avoid those time-consuming fairway faux pas.

The Faux Pas: Not ready when it's your turn.

The Solution: As you approach your ball, begin to look for the signs you need to determine how your next shot will be played; yardage markers, hazards, and possible ways to approach the green can all indicate what you need to do next; don't wait until it's your turn to start considering these factors.

The Faux Pas: Taking too long to find lost ball.

The Solution: If one person hits while the others look for the ball, it will speed things up; if the spot was properly marked off the tee, you'll zero in on the ball more easily; the rules give you up to 5 minutes, but they aren't counting on you losing a ball every hole, so keep the searches short.

The Faux Pas: Taking too long to make a shot.

The Solution: Develop a quick pre-shot routine that enables you to assess your shot, take a practice swing, and then step up and hit the ball; you'll hit with more confidence and you'll play more quickly.

The Faux Pas: Golf carts slow down the play.

The Solution: First, don't drive to one ball then wait while that player prepares then hits; drop player number one off then drive to your ball, and let player number one walk to the cart after hitting. Second, when the rule is "cart path only," make sure you take extra clubs to your shot so you don't waste time walking back and forth.

Remember to balance your ready golf with the safety rules: do not get in front of someone who is hitting, and always be aware if someone might be in your line of fire before you hit.

Waltzing On the Dance Floor

Fully half the shots that are designated for par are hit on the greens. That means half the game takes place on the green, so there are lots of places where the game could slow down if you're not careful.

Your pace-of-play duties begin even before you get to the green. As you approach the green, begin to look for ridges and undulations that may influence the path of your putt. Leave your bag or cart on the side of the green from which you will exit to the next hole.

Then observe some simple techniques of making your stay on the green a short but positive visit.

- Ask if anyone needs the flag tended. If not, place the flag off to the side of the green. If the flag does need to be tended, have the person whose ball is closest to the hole tend the pin.

- Line up your putt while someone else is hitting his or hers; don't wait until it's your turn before you start thinking about which way your putt goes.

- Putt out any real shorties you have left; don't mark your ball and putt again later.

- Don't take practice putts after you have holed out.

Once your group has completed the hole, replace the flag and move directly off the green. As noted earlier, don't stand around tallying and marking scores. Do that on the next tee. Keep in mind that golf etiquette is not only about the people who are in your group; it is about all the people who are behind you, too.

Keeping Up With the Bobby Joneses

Keep up with the group ahead of you (within half a hole).

Be ready when it is your turn.

Assess your upcoming shot as you approach your ball.

Play ready golf.

Establish a quick pre-shot routine.

On the tee, watch everyone's shot, and help look for lost balls.

Line up your putt while others are putting.

Playing Through with Grace

There is probably no area of golf that is more liable to be contentious than when one group wants to play through another group. If a single golfer wants to play through a foursome and there is no one ahead, there is usually no problem (unless the single has been too pushy and the foursome decides to resist). But if a foursome wants to play through a foursome, there could be trouble brewing.

Playing through brings up the same emotions as when someone is driving less than the speed limit in the left lane of a busy freeway. Some drivers might respond a bit more aggressively than others and it can lead to all kinds of road-rage stories in the headlines.

Many battles have been waged over this exact scenario on the highways and byways of America. And the same battles are often staged on the golf courses of America as well. But communication between foursomes can be more easily facilitated than while you are hurtling along at 70 mph.

Just like on the highway, where ramming someone from behind is probably not the most productive course of action, it is never acceptable to send a message to the group ahead in the form of a "hurry up" golf ball. It might produce results that you did not anticipate.

Understanding that there are two perspectives to consider in this particular human interaction, the "passer" and the "passee," here are some things to consider regarding playing through.

If you are the passer:

- Be sure there is room ahead of the group through whom you wish to play—if they are being held up, too, then playing through them doesn't do anyone any good.

- Ask politely if you can play through at the next convenient hole—sometimes the only place to do it conveniently is at the turn, but playing through at a par 3 can work well, too.

- When you get ahead, make sure you play at a good pace—nothing is worse than having a group play through and then they all hit balls OB and spend all afternoon looking for them.

If you are the passee:

- If you see that you are more than one hole behind the group ahead of you, and the group behind is often left waiting to hit their shots, then volunteer to let them play through—that is the best golf etiquette.
- If a group asks to play through and it seems reasonable, be gracious and let them do so; then make an effort to keep up with them so you don't hold up the next group, too.

Playing through at a par 3 can be quite easy if you follow a simple procedure:

- The first group hits their shots off the tee and proceeds to their balls; assuming you did not all hit the green with your first shots (and this is part of why you are so slow), continue to hit until all balls are on the green.
- Mark the golf balls on the green, step to the side of the green, and wave up the next group.
- After they have hit their shots and are proceeding to the green, the first group putts out and moves to the next tee where they wait until the next group has putted out.

- Let the passers hit their tee shots, and when they have played ahead to a safe distance, then the passees can hit and proceed forward.

- Some people suggest that the passees can hit together with the passers and move together into the fairway, but I think that creates too much of a crowd in the fairway.

Remember as you think about your responsibility in terms of pace of play: if you are a bogey golfer (e.g., you generally hit a score of 90) and you take 1 extra minute before each shot, then you have just added an hour and a half to your round of golf—and to the round of golf for everyone behind you for the rest of the day. Be considerate. Play quickly.

The Least You Need to Know

- Play ready golf, which recognizes that regardless of who scored best on the previous hole, the player who is ready to hit is allowed to while the other is busy getting ready.

- When on the tee, choose correct tees for your game, mark where all shots went, and hit a provisional ball if it is likely your ball is lost.

- When in the fairway, pay attention and be ready when it's your turn, don't look too long for lost balls, and develop a quick and effective pre-shot routine.

- When on the green, line up putts while others are hitting theirs, leave bags and carts near the proper exit of the green, and mark your scores on the next tee, not on the green.

- Playing through can be easy if you are courteous and reasonable.

Chapter 5

Penalties

In This Chapter

- The stakes are high: white, yellow, and red
- Penalties in a hazard
- Lost but not forgotten
- Provisional ball
- Unplayable lie
- Wrong ball

Virtually every game has penalties. In football, penalties are meted out in lost yards; in basketball, it's loss of the ball or free throws for the other team; in hockey, they actually have a penalty box where they give you a "time out."

Penalties in golf are punished with extra strokes or loss of the hole depending on the format you play. Sometimes there is a combination of penalty strokes with an extra twist of yardage, too (called *stroke and distance*). It may be hard to remember this as you are extricating your ball from yet another *unplayable lie*, but penalty strokes make a lot of sense. Without them there would be no way to differentiate between a player who hits the ball to a good lie and one who doesn't.

So then, we're agreed. If you put the ball in a place from which it cannot be hit again, you deserve a penalty stroke to put it back in play. Here are some of the more common penalties that the average (and even the above-average) golfer encounters. And just as important, here is what you need to do with the ball before you hit it again.

A Stake Through the Heart

Every once in a while golfers have a problem with geography. The problem is, they run out of it. There are areas of the golf course that have been designated by *white stakes*, *yellow stakes*, or *red stakes* and that usually spell trouble for the unfortunate player who has gone boldly where no golfer wants to go.

White Stakes—Out of Bounds

The size of the average golf course is 120 acres for urban courses and up to 190 acres for resort courses. The golf ball is only 1.68 inches in diameter. So, why is it so hard to find a spot within 190 acres to land such a small object? Somehow people find ways to get their ball out of bounds.

The white stakes define the area known as out of bounds, or "OB" to those of us with a great deal of experience in this terrain. The penalty for hitting your ball OB is pretty cut and dried: it is called "stroke and distance." You can neither play your ball from OB, nor can you take a drop along the course near where your ball exited the premises.

Did You Know That?

Your ball is OB when the entire ball is out. So if one dimple is still in, you can play that ball with no penalty. Yippee!

Stroke and distance means you must play another stroke from the place you just hit (to cover that distance again) and count a penalty stroke. Okay, you tee off and slice one beyond the fence to an area that is clearly OB; so you tee up another ball and when that ball is sitting on the tee, it lies 2; then you hit that ball and it lies 3. Welcome to stroke and distance.

But let's say you hit the second ball OB, too. Okay, you tee up another, which lies 4 on the tee, and hit that ball, which, when it lands somewhere, lies 5. And so on until such time that you either land one where it can legally be hit or you decide that perhaps bowling is more suited to your talents.

The same penalty applies to any ball that is hit OB, whether it is hit off the tee or from the fairway. Many times the line for OB runs along an entire hole (marked by white stakes, a line on the ground or a fence of some kind). If you shank one out of the fairway and it goes OB, you must drop a ball as near as possible to the spot you just hit from and hit again (good old stroke and distance).

Did You Know That?

When OB is marked by a white line, the line itself is out of bounds. When OB is marked by stakes, you have to eyeball it along a straight line between the inside edge of the stakes.

Yellow Stakes–Water Hazard

Yellow stakes or yellow lines on the course mark a *water hazard*, which generally indicates water that crosses into the fairway. And when you hit into a yellow-staked area, there are a few choices available to you. Depending on the situation, they are not all bad.

Did You Know That?

On the fifteenth hole at Augusta in the 1974 Masters, Jack Nicklaus landed his second shot just in the water, right in front of the green. From knee-deep in the water he blasted the ball out to within a couple of inches of the hole and made birdie!

Sometimes in a water hazard, there is an area between the hazard marks (the stakes or lines) and where the water actually begins. That means you might realistically have a shot, even though you are technically in the hazard. And it is even possible to have a shot if your ball is right in the water.

If you do have a shot at the ball, you can take it with no penalty strokes. But if you can't hit the ball, then you have two other options:

- Hit another ball from the spot where you just previously hit, and count a penalty stroke (stroke and distance).

- Create an imaginary line between the hole and the place where your ball last crossed the margin of the water hazard; drop the ball any place on that line behind the hazard as far back away from the hole as you want to go. And when you drop the ball, add one penalty stroke.

If you decide to play out of the hazard, remember that *grounding your club in the hazard* is a penalty. And that includes touching the water with your club as you set up for your shot or during your backswing. Your first contact with the hazard must be made on your forward swing.

Red Stakes–Lateral Water Hazard

Red stakes or red lines on the course signify *lateral water hazards*, and by the name you can tell they generally run alongside the fairway or other parts of the course. And just like with the yellow stakes, you may find that you have a shot from within the staked area. If so, you may take that shot without a penalty.

If you cannot hit the ball from within the hazard, then you have some options to consider:

- Hit another ball from the spot where you just previously hit, and count a penalty stroke (stroke and distance).

- Depending on the way the hazard is situated, create an imaginary line between the hole and the place where the ball just crossed into the hazard; drop the ball any place on that line behind the hazard as far back away from the hole as you want to go. (Depending on the layout of the hazard, this option might not be available.) And when you drop the ball, add one penalty stroke.

- Drop a ball to the side of the hazard, within two club lengths of the spot where the ball last crossed the margin of the hazard, but not closer to the hole. Take a penalty stroke.

- Drop a ball on the opposite side of the hazard from where the ball last crossed the margin of the hazard, within two club lengths, and of course, not closer to the hole. Ah yes, don't forget that penalty stroke.

Just to underscore that the rules have a heart, you are not penalized if your club or hands touch the ground as the result of your trying to prevent falling down. Isn't that swell?

Hazardous Penalties

Being in a hazard is bad enough, and in many cases presents a very difficult shot for the amateur golfer to face. But to make matters even worse, there are some special penalties associated with a ball in the hazard. First and foremost, golfers need to understand that these rules apply to sand bunkers as well as to water hazards (either red or yellow), so extra care should be taken in those areas.

There are three things to watch out for and avoid when your ball is in anything defined as a hazard:

- Don't *test the conditions* in your hazard, or any other hazard nearby.
- Don't touch the ground with your hand or your club.
- Don't remove *loose impediment*, such as stones or twigs, within the hazard.

Testing the conditions of a hazard, particularly a sand bunker, can consist of many things. And since testing is not within the spirit of "playing the ball as it lies," the rules are pretty rigid about what constitutes testing. They don't want golfers testing the limits on testing the conditions.

If you go into the bunker and start kicking sand around to decide if it is soft and loose, or wet and hard, then clearly you are testing the conditions. But you are allowed to set your feet firmly in the sand; so if you wiggle your feet around to get a fair stance, that is okay. You are also prohibited from testing the conditions in a nearby similar hazard.

Did You Know That?

If you wiggle your feet into the sand and then walk over to your bag to get a different club, you can come back and wiggle again without violating the rule for testing the conditions.

When you *address the ball* in a hazard, you are not allowed to ground the club before your swing. And according to the rules, the swing just includes the downswing; so that means you cannot touch the ground (or the sand) on your backswing.

You are also not allowed to remove loose impediment from behind your ball when your ball is in a hazard. However, you are allowed to remove *movable obstructions* and that would include things like litter or other human-made objects.

Did You Know That?

In the 2006 Women's British Open, Michelle Wie was penalized two strokes because her club made contact with a piece of moss in a greenside bunker during her backswing.

Keep in mind that local rules may allow you to remove stones from sand bunkers as a safety precaution. This local rule is designed to prevent stones from flying out of a bunker and hitting another player. Check the scorecard for this.

Lost Ball: Bye, Bye Birdie!

Losing a golf ball can be a very sad experience—especially if it's the fifth or sixth one for that day. Each one seems to make you sadder. It's not just the *lost golf balls* you mourn; it's the strokes associated with them that can be so disheartening.

But a lot of people seem to misunderstand the rule for how to score a lost ball. Many times they simply drop a ball near the area where the lost ball was last seen and take a penalty stroke. But that is not correct. The actual penalty for a lost ball is our old friend, stroke and distance.

Let's say you are looking at a fairway that has a deep forest along the left side and a marshy area filled with trees along the right side. (Whew! You've got to start playing somewhere else; this place is tough.) The left side of the fairway that has the deep forest has no markings of any kind, but the right side with the marsh has red stakes along the fairway.

Now, one member of your group slices a ball into the marsh and trees, but you hook your ball to the other side and it goes way into the deep forest. I have bad news. The guy in the red-staked area is going to get to drop his ball within two club lengths of the place where his ball crossed into the hazard. But you are not.

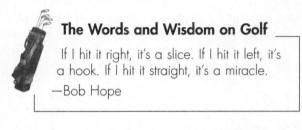

The Words and Wisdom on Golf

If I hit it right, it's a slice. If I hit it left, it's a hook. If I hit it straight, it's a miracle.
—Bob Hope

Your ball is *lost outside of a hazard*, therefore you must play it as a stroke and distance penalty. Since the ball is clearly lost, you must play your next shot from the previous spot, whether that was from the tee or the fairway.

Hope Springs Eternal

Okay, so far in this chapter you've been hitting a lot of balls where they don't belong. I think it's time you hit one straight. And there is no better time for that than when you are hitting your provisional ball.

The provisional ball is a concession in the rules to saving time and keeping pace with the group ahead of you. If a golfer had to chase down and look for every ball before determining it was lost, then proceed back to the tee to hit another, it could require a lot of extra time. If it happened too often, the group behind would justifiably become very unhappy and impatient.

So the rules allow you to hit another shot, which you can use "provided" you do not find the first one. You only need to hit a provisional ball if it is unclear that your ball is lost. If you see it splash into the lake, then you know you should proceed under the appropriate water hazard rule. But if it went in the direction of some trouble that is not in a hazard (e.g., long grass or rough) and it might be lost, then the provisional ball is in order.

The way you proceed under a provisional ball is as follows:

- Announce your intention to hit a provisional ball.

- Hit the provisional ball.

- You may continue to hit the provisional ball until you are roughly up to the spot where your original, lost ball might be located.

- Look for your lost ball.

- If you find it, you must play the original ball under whatever rules apply, and discontinue play with the provisional ball.

- If, after a search of no more than 5 minutes, you determine the original is lost, the provisional ball becomes your *ball in play*. Of course, you must add a penalty stroke.

- There is no penalty stroke if you find the original ball within five minutes and it is playable.

Let's say you're having a tough day. You don't find your original ball, but you hit your provisional ball into the water; then you must take the stroke for the original lost ball and play the provisional ball under the appropriate water-hazard rule.

What happens if you hit your provisional ball into the exact same spot as your original ball? Therefore you think the provisional ball might be lost, too. Announce you are hitting a second provisional ball and proceed. If you find the first ball, you are lucky because you must play that one.

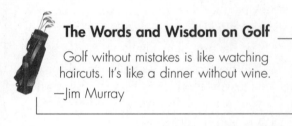

The Words and Wisdom on Golf

Golf without mistakes is like watching haircuts. It's like a dinner without wine.
—Jim Murray

If you can't find the original ball but you find provisional ball number one, then you must use that. If you can't find either of those but you find provisional ball number two, then you must play that. If you can't find any of them, then you must go back and hit again from the previous spot, taking penalty strokes for each ball. Then proceed under stroke and distance until you finally hit something you can find. May I suggest you try a different club?

Findable—But Not Playable

Unplayable lies come in all shapes and forms, and no one knows this better than the amateur golfer. Balls up in trees, balls in the middle of bushes, balls in the rock gardens, and this is all on one hole!

The good news about the unplayable lie is that you, and you alone, get to determine that your lie is unplayable. The bad news is that you can't just throw it down anywhere that you decide is playable. And this is a mistake that lots of amateurs make.

Very often you see a weekend golfer hit a ball into some deep woods, and after some thrashing about in the briars and brambles, he comes out with a ball somewhat resembling the one he hit in there. He'll say, "That one was unplayable so I am going to take a drop out here, where it is playable." Sorry.

Did You Know That?

The designation of "unplayable" defines a particular spot, not a general area. So if you take a drop, it must be measured from the exact spot at which you determined it was unplayable.

That is not one of the options available to you for an unplayable lie, but there are three options that you can consider.

- Hit another ball from the spot you hit before the ball became unplayable and count a penalty stroke (stroke and distance).

- Create an imaginary line between the hole and the spot where the unplayable ball is located; drop the ball any place on that line behind the spot as far back away from the hole as you want to go. When you drop the ball, add one penalty stroke.

- Drop a ball within two club lengths of the spot where the ball is situated, but not closer to the hole. Add one penalty stroke.

If your unplayable lie is up in a tree or otherwise not on the ground, you measure the two club lengths from the spot on the ground directly under where the ball is situated. Frequently the best option for an unplayable lie is to go back and play from the previous spot.

A Case of Mistaken Identity

Sometimes it seems almost any ball is better than the one that you have to hit. So it is understandable that, from time to time, one might have a tendency to hit the *wrong ball*. But most times, hitting a wrong ball is done totally by accident. Imagine that.

The rule on playing a wrong ball distinguishes between a ball in a hazard and outside a hazard.

The Words and Wisdom on Golf

If you think it's hard to meet new people, try picking up the wrong golf ball.

—Jack Lemmon

Within a hazard:

- There is no penalty.
- Strokes made at the wrong ball don't count in the score.
- The player must go back and play the correct ball.
- If a player fails to correct the mistake before teeing off on the next hole, she is disqualified.

Outside a hazard:

- There is a two-stroke penalty (loss of hole in match play).
- Strokes made at the wrong ball don't count in the score.
- The player must go back and play the correct ball.

The reason for the difference in results from playing inside or outside a hazard is easy to understand. Under a different rule of golf, the player is allowed to lift a ball to identify it, unless the ball is in a hazard. So since the identity of the ball in a hazard may be unclear, you are not penalized if you hit the wrong ball. See, the rules are reasonable.

If the ball you played belonged to another player (as opposed to an abandoned ball you stumbled upon), the other player may place a ball at the spot where the mistake took place. If you found and played someone else's abandoned ball by mistake, you must find your own and play that one once you realize a mistake has been made.

A word of warning: do not take someone else's word regarding which ball is yours. Always check for yourself. If someone else says, "This one is mine and that one is yours," she may be wrong. And if you hit that wrong ball, you incur the penalty.

The Least You Need to Know

- White stakes mean out of bounds. The penalty is stroke and distance.
- Yellow stakes are a water hazard. You have three options: if playable, hit without penalty; stroke and distance; drop on a straight line behind hazard, one stroke.
- Red stakes mean a lateral water hazard. You have five options: if playable, hit without penalty; stroke and distance; drop on a straight line behind hazard, one stroke; drop two club lengths to the side of entry point, one stroke; drop two club lengths on opposite side of entry point, one stroke.
- You will be assessed a hazard penalty if you test the conditions of a hazard; make sure you don't ground your club in a hazard.

- For a lost ball (not in a hazard) the penalty is stroke and distance. For an unplayable lie, you decide if it is unplayable. You have three options: stroke and distance; drop on a straight line behind unplayable lie; drop two club lengths out, not nearer the hole.

- Hit a provisional if your ball may be lost outside of a hazard; if you find the original ball, you must play that; if not, the provisional ball becomes your ball in play. If you hit the wrong ball, there is no penalty if in a hazard; two strokes if outside a hazard.

How Do You Spell Free Relief?

In This Chapter

- Obstructions (movable and unmovable)
- Casual water/ground under repair
- Swallowed by the earth—an embedded ball
- Right idea, wrong green
- Loose impediments
- Ball moved by ball

When it comes to penalty strokes, the USGA giveth and the USGA taketh away. Chapter 5 was a whole lot of giveth, but this chapter is an equal measure of taketh away.

The rules of the game recognize that there are certain situations in which it's entirely reasonable to allow the golfer to pick up and move a ball without penalty, despite the basic rule of play it as it lies. Those situations generally occur through no fault of the golfer and surround things the golfer could not anticipate or control. When golfers are allowed by the rules to pick up and move a ball without penalty, it is referred to as free relief.

Moving Heaven and Earth

Golf courses rose up from the fields and meadows of medieval Scotland and contained nothing but the elements and objects one would expect in a natural setting. But as the game became more modern and sophisticated, along came things like sprinkler systems and electrical boxes that occasionally block a shot.

The rules allow some leeway when it comes to those obstructions. There are two types of such obstructions and you will encounter both as you wind your way around the links.

Movable Obstructions

Movable obstructions might be encountered in a variety of forms around the golf course. Rakes for the bunkers can block a ball, litter that might be around the course could come into play, a waste-paper basket might get in the way, and any number of other unanticipated objects could become obstructions. Because they are movable, there is an easy solution to the problem: move them. But the way you do it can be very important.

- Blocked by the obstruction: if your ball is neither in nor on the obstruction, but is merely being blocked by it, then you can simply move the obstruction and play your ball as it lies.

- In or on the obstruction: if the ball is in or on the obstruction, e.g., inside a waste-paper basket, then you can remove the ball, move the obstruction, and drop the ball onto the ground directly below where it had been in the obstruction.

If your ball is blocked, be careful to mark the ball before you move the obstruction. That way, if the ball moves when you take away the object, you can replace the ball back to its original spot.

Did You Know That?

During the 2006 U.S. Open, Phil Michelson hit his drive on the seventeenth hole into a garbage bag in the rough. But he was able to remove the ball from the garbage bag and take a drop. Sadly, he was not able to extract his game from the garbage bag, as he double bogied the eighteenth to sacrifice the lead and the victory.

If your ball happens to be on the green when it is blocked by the obstruction, you place the ball rather than dropping it. You would place it as near as possible to its original spot, and not closer to the hole. Again, it is always a safe strategy to mark the ball if possible before you remove the obstruction.

Immovable Obstructions

One of the age-old dilemmas of Philosophy 101 is this: what happens when an irresistible force meets an immovable object? "Ah!" you say, "This is a trick question, because by definition, there can be no universe in which an irresistible force and an immovable object coexist."

But that was before you understood the rules of golf. Now you realize that when the irresistible force of a golfer, who is determined to avoid a triple bogey, meets the immovable object of, say … a water fountain, there is a solution. And what's even better, it comes with no penalty strokes.

As it turns out, a golfer could encounter many *immovable obstructions* around the course, contrary to the tenets of Philosophy 101. Things like guy-wires supporting trees or sign posts, paved or concrete roads, cart paths and wooden steps leading up to tee boxes, are all immovable obstructions from which you can get free relief.

Did You Know That?

The free relief from immovable obstructions applies to the golfer's stance and area of intended swing. It does not, however, include the intended line of play. So if your ball is behind a barn but your swing is not blocked and your stance is not blocked, then you can't claim the free relief from the barn as an immovable obstruction. You must play around it.

It's important to remember that, even though you are entitled to relief, it is not always as much as you might wish for. You have to take your drop at the *nearest point of relief,* not your favorite point of relief, or the most beneficial point of relief. Here is how it works in real life. You can get free relief from immovable obstructions:

- Through the green: within one club length of the nearest point of relief, not closer to the hole

- In a bunker: a) without penalty, within one club length of the nearest point of relief (nearest point must be in the bunker and the ball must be dropped in the bunker) or b) with a one-stroke penalty, outside the bunker anywhere on a straight line between where the ball is and the hole, as far back behind the bunker as you want to go

- On the green: lift and place the ball at the nearest point of relief not nearer the hole (nearest point may be off the green)

If you are on the green, you can get relief from an immovable obstruction, like a sprinkler head, which may block the line of your putt. Elsewhere on the course you cannot get relief just because the line of your shot is blocked. The difference is that the line of your putt is along the ground but, hopefully, the lines of your other shots are not.

The most common close encounter that golfers have with immovable objects is when the ball lands on a cart path. You may also get relief if the cart path blocks your stance or area of intended swing. So let's take a simple look at how to get yourself back into the swing of things when that occurs:

- First locate the nearest point of relief that is not closer to the hole.
- Mark the nearest point of relief; if your ball is more than halfway to one side, your nearest point of relief is most likely on that side.
- Measure one club length from the mark.
- Drop the ball in that one-club-length area, no closer to the hole.
- You're set to go.

As you play more and more golf you will surely encounter lots of immovable obstructions, but they should not pose any great problems to you. Just be sure no matter how many immovable obstructions you encounter in your round, that you are always an irresistible force for good golf and good golf etiquette.

One If By Land, Two If By Sea

Casual water and *ground under repair* are categories of temporary interference that golfers encounter from time to time. Casual water is simply a puddle, large or small, that might collect in a depression in a fairway or bunker. A lake is not casual water—it is more formal water.

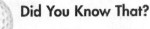

Did You Know That?

Frost and morning dew on the grass are not considered casual water.

Golf courses are often like works of art in their design and manufacture, but they are works of art that sometimes need to have the sprinklers fixed. So you may run into some mounds of dirt or other areas that are clearly being improved in one way or another. Those areas are typically marked with a sign or flag to indicate they are ground under repair and that the golfer is entitled to a free lift.

If your ball is through the green and lands in casual water or ground under repair (GUR), you may drop it within one club length of the nearest point of relief, as long as it is not closer to the hole.

If you're on the green and get stuck in casual water or blocked by GUR, you may place your ball at the closest spot that eliminates the interference but is not closer to the hole.

You've Made Your Embed, Now Lie in It

On a soggy day of golf in the winter or early spring months, it is possible to hit a shot high up into the air and have it splat down, seemingly into the center of the earth. Okay, raise your hands: how many readers have actually lost their shot right in the fairway from an *embedded ball*? Golf is tough.

But golf has its aspects of fairness, too. If you find your ball and it's embedded in the ground, you may be able to get a free drop. The reason I say "may" be able to is because in order for you to get the free relief, the ball must be embedded in the short grass known as a closely mown area, through the green. And when you think about that, it makes sense; the rules are acknowledging a good shot that, without the soggy conditions, would have been perfect.

A ball in the rough, however, is not deserving of the same reward, and therefore, you get no relief for that one. Alas, the golf gods are not very forgiving.

Did You Know That?

The benefit of a free lift is only conferred upon those balls landing in the closely mown areas, including the fairway and anything mowed to the level of the fairway or less.

If you are fortunate enough to find your ball embedded in the short grass, you may lift that ball out, clean it, and drop it as near as possible to the spot where it had embedded but not closer to the hole.

You should not fix the hole the ball was embedded in before you drop the ball. That would violate the rule against improving your lie. But if your ball, when dropped, ends up in the previous hole or a hole created during the drop, you may drop the ball again.

The Eagle Has Landed—On the Wrong Green

One of the goals in golf is to get the ball onto the green in regulation, but a very important consideration is to get the ball onto the right green. After all, it's even harder to accept 3-putting on the *wrong green*.

But in the event that you end up on the wrong green, there is at least some good news: you get a free lift. In fact, in most other instances of relief, you have the option to take the relief. But when you are on the wrong green you *must* take the relief. This rule makes perfect sense, since the last thing any golf course would want is to have golfers hacking into the surface of the greens with their seven-irons in an attempt to get across two fairways and back onto their own green.

Did You Know That?

The free lift for being on the wrong green does not include the situation where your stance is on the wrong green, only when your ball is on the wrong green.

So the way you handle a ball on the wrong green is simple. You take your standard drop within one club length of the nearest point of relief, which is generally going to be on an apron somewhere around the green but not nearer the hole you are actually aiming for. Remember that the nearest point of relief means you don't get to choose which direction you will opt for; you may end up hitting across that wrong green on your way to the correct green. Please make sure no one is putting before you do.

Pick-Up Sticks

Have you ever played a game of "pick-up sticks"? You have to carefully pick one stick up out of the pile of sticks without moving any of the other sticks. It's nerve-wracking and tense work that takes a steady hand and a keen eye. If you bump something by accident, you lose. Welcome to the world of loose impediments.

What exactly does loose impediment mean? The term describes the little flotsam and jetsam that might be lying around the ground that would prevent you from making clean contact with your ball. Things that qualify as loose impediments are sticks, stones, pinecones, leaves, and other such stuff. The good news is you are allowed to lift the loose impediment away from your ball. The bad news is if you move your ball in the process, you incur a penalty stroke; so you must be very careful in this game of pick-up sticks.

Did You Know That?

Tiger Woods hit his ball behind a giant boulder in a natural waste area in a tournament. (By the way, a natural waste area is not designated as a hazard.) He asked if it could be considered loose impediment, and the on-site official agreed that it was. So Tiger had a bunch of spectators roll the giant stone out of the way so he could hit his shot. Knowing the rules really helps.

Loose impediment cannot be removed when your ball is in a hazard. You remember from earlier that you cannot touch the ground with either your club or your hand, so removing the loose impediment would be very difficult under those circumstances.

Did You Know That?

Local rules will often allow you to remove stones from sand bunkers as loose impediment. Depending on the type of sand they use in the bunkers, this could be a safety factor; they don't want large stones flying out of the bunkers and hitting people standing nearby. Check the scorecard at the course to see if this is allowed.

Golf Balls On the Move

There is a widely accepted rule of physics that two things cannot occupy the same space at the same time. There is a very similar rule in golf. So if your ball is sitting pretty, waiting for you to come and hit it again, and out of the clear blue sky another ball comes along and bangs into it, something's got to give.

Because of another rule of physics, something to do with equal and opposite reactions, usually what happens is that both balls fly off in roughly opposite directions. Keep an eye on that spot because your ball is coming back there very soon.

The solution is simple: the ball that had been at rest is moved back and placed as near as possible to the original spot before it was moved. The ball that moved it is simply played from wherever it landed (played as it lies). No penalties for anyone.

Did You Know That?

There is an exception to this situation that does include a penalty: if a ball in motion hits a ball that is in play and at rest, and both balls were on the green prior to the shot, then the player whose stroke hit the ball at rest gets a two-stroke penalty. Ouch.

The laws of physics and gravity come into play a lot as you try to get that little white ball into the cup. And if those laws team up with the rules of golf to let you move your ball back where it was with no penalty, how can that be bad?

The Least You Need to Know

- Movable obstructions can be moved without penalty; if the obstruction blocks the ball, then simply move the obstruction; if the ball is in or on the obstruction, move the obstruction then drop the ball to the spot on the ground under the obstruction.

- Immovable obstructions require you to take a drop within one club length of the nearest point of relief, no closer to the hole.

- Interference from casual water or ground under repair allows you to drop a ball at the nearest point of relief, no closer to the hole.

- An embedded ball in the closely mown areas of the course can be dropped as close as possible to the spot where it was embedded, no nearer the hole.

- If your ball comes to rest on the wrong green, you must drop the ball at the nearest point of relief, not nearer the hole to which you are playing.

- Loose impediments can be moved from around your ball, but not if your ball is in a hazard. Do not move the ball in the process of moving the impediments or you will incur a penalty stroke.

- If your ball at rest is moved by another ball, replace your ball as close as possible to its original spot. The other ball is played from wherever it comes to rest; unless both balls were on the green when the stroke was made, in which case the player who struck the stationary ball receives a two-stroke penalty.

Chapter 7

On the Green

In This Chapter

- Repairing your ball mark
- Marking your ball
- Line of the putt
- Around the hole
- Tending the flagstick
- Going to school

The green is a special place to golfers. It is the holy of holies, the inner sanctum of the game. In a round of even par, the green is the place where half of all your strokes will be taken. And the strokes taken here are fraught with peril. In the fairway you can miss your target (the middle of the fairway) by 10 or 15 yards and still be in perfect shape for your next shot. But on the green, a miss by 1 inch can be a huge disappointment.

The rules and the etiquette of golf have evolved over centuries of the game to protect the green and support the attempts by golfers to experience the highest level of success and satisfaction. The often-elaborate rituals that are performed on the green demonstrate the extent to which golfers understand and respect the task ahead for themselves and their playing partners.

Let's explore some of those rituals to see how golf is played on the greens.

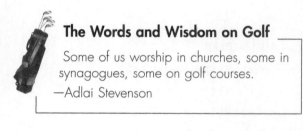

The Words and Wisdom on Golf

Some of us worship in churches, some in synagogues, some on golf courses.
—Adlai Stevenson

Don't Leave a Bad Impression

One of the truly joyful experiences in golf is watching a shot you just hit arc across a blue sky, fly toward a wind-whipped flag, bite into the emerald surface of the green, and settle into position for a birdie. Of course, three putts later that joy may be a distant memory, but it was fun while it lasted.

Not every golfer out on the course has the skill to create that shot. It takes a lot of practice and a significant amount of skill to pull that off. So as you stroll, with great satisfaction, to survey your lie, take pride in your accomplishment. Upon closer inspection, you will see your ball did take a big bite out of the green. And now comes the part in which you can take the greatest pride: fixing the ball mark you just made with your terrific shot.

Did You Know That?

According to the rules, it is acceptable, when your ball is on the green, to repair a ball mark that is on the line of your putt—whether it's your mark or one made by another golfer.

Every good golfer will carry in his pocket a ball mark repair tool and will use it generously throughout the round. The technique for repairing the ball mark is simple. And if care is taken, the surface of the green will not show any blemish when you are finished, and the grass will restore itself quickly and completely.

Here's what to do:

- Look at the mark and notice that when the ball landed, it compressed a tuft of grass to the back of the mark and created a depression in the middle (because the ball came in at an angle, not straight down).
- Place your ball mark repair tool at the back of the mark and gently unfold the compressed grass out over that depression.
- Use your ball mark repair tool to gently straighten out the sides of the mark until it is even all around.

- Gently tamp it down with your foot or the head of your putter to smooth it out; when you are finished, you should not be able to tell whether any damage was done.

Any job worth doing is worth doing well. So avoid the technique whereby you jam the tool in and yank it around, resulting in the soil from below being brought to the surface, leaving a big brown splotch on the surface of the green.

As a conscientious golfer, you should make certain you have accounted for any marks you have made on the green. But as one who truly loves the game, you should be on the lookout for the marks others have made but left unrepaired. Bend down and fix one or two of those as well as your own. If every golfer fixed her own and a couple of others, the greens would always provide an elegant carpet on which to roll perfect putts. (Of course, if every golfer fixed her own mark, there wouldn't be any others.)

Making Your Mark in the World

Once your ball is safely on the green and you are getting ready to putt, the rules of golf provide you the option to pick up your ball and clean it. The procedure to do so is simple, but too often the amateur golfer will botch the process in a way that, according to the rules, should cost two strokes. You will see the inexperienced golfer (1) pick up the ball, then (2) place the marker in the exact spot that was, moments ago, occupied by the ball.

He has the right idea, but the wrong order of events. The ball must be marked *before* it can be lifted (remember the earlier discussion about the ball being in play until it is marked). The rules suggest that a small token, like a coin, should be used to mark the ball, and it is generally placed behind the ball. Then when the ball is put back into play, the ball simply goes in front of the marker, on the exact spot from which it was taken. Then the marker is removed, and everything is copasetic.

Did You Know That?

From the beginning of the game of golf until 1951, golfers did not mark the ball on the green. The ball was left wherever it came to rest and other golfers had to either putt around or over any ball in the way. That situation was called a *stymie*.

Some people foolishly place their markers in front of the ball (i.e. between the ball and the hole). That is a bad idea for one very important reason: it could make an impression on the line of your putt, which will make it more difficult for you to putt straight.

If the ball marker is inadvertently moved in the process of replacing the ball, simply resituate the marker before replacing the ball (without penalty). If the player moves the ball marker while not in the process of replacing the ball, a penalty stroke is incurred.

Moving Your Ball

As you survey the location of your ball on the green, you may find it is sitting right in the line someone else is planning to use for her putt. Consequently, you may be asked to move your ball to one side or the other to prevent their ball from hitting your mark and deflecting it off course on its way to the hole. No problem.

Here's all you need to do:

- Be sure your ball is marked first.
- Place the head of your putter alongside your ball mark at a 90-degree angle to the putting line.
- Move the mark to the other end of your putter-head where it will be out of the way of the oncoming putt.
- Depending on the amount of break expected from the putt, the other golfer may ask you to move your mark the length of two putter heads to be sure it is out of the way.
- Be sure to return your mark to its original position before you putt.

When asked to move your ball so another person can putt on the line you occupy, be sure to mark your ball first, and then move the mark. When you are replacing the ball, you should actually replace the mark, and then put the ball back into its original position.

Did You Know That?

When using your putter to move your mark off someone's line, it's a good idea to point your putter at some fixed position nearby. Then, when you return your mark you can use the same landmark to identify the precise spot you had originally occupied.

Moving your ball (actually, your mark) is a simple courtesy, but be sure you do it correctly so you do not incur any penalty strokes.

I Walk the Line

Putting is such a crucial part of the game of golf and so nerve-wracking that the rules of golf have several special accommodations just dealing with the line of your putt. As discussed earlier, a golfer cannot take any action to impact the line of play while anywhere on the golf course. However, on the green the line of play is along the ground, and it is much easier to affect that line. So the rules are quite a bit more precise.

The rule prohibiting touching the line is, no doubt, designed to prevent golfers from digging a trench or creating a depression that will go from their ball straight into the hole. And since most rules are the by-product of experience, it means someone has probably already tried that trick in the past. (Obviously, some knucklehead has gone and ruined it for the rest of us.)

Did You Know That?

When caddies are showing their golfers where the line of the putt goes, they will point to the target line, but they never actually touch it.

But we must follow the rules as they are, so let's see what we can and can't do with the line of our putt.

Here's what you can do:

- You can remove loose impediment from your line. (So if Tiger has that gigantic boulder moved from his line of play and it rolls onto your putting line, you can have all of your fans move it for you).

- Place your putter in front of your ball in the process of lining up your putt; but don't press down in a way that might imply you are trying to affect your line.

- You can repair a ball mark from a previous golfer or one that you made (or a mound or depression from a *previous hole placement*).

- You can remove a movable obstruction, like litter or a nasty old cigar butt.

And here's what you can't do:

- Touch the line in any way that might influence the path your ball travels.
- Fix spike marks carelessly made by someone's golf shoes.
- Set up to putt your ball by either straddling the line of your putt or standing with either foot on the line of your putt.

Stepping Over the Ball Path

The line of a putt is so important that golfers do not want other golfers standing or walking on their line. There are just so many things that can go wrong between the moment the ball leaves the face of your putter and when it takes that last 5-inch break to the bottom of the cup.

In order to assuage your playing partners and demonstrate the extent of your fine golf etiquette, the first thing you should do when you walk onto a green is make a note of where all the other golf balls are situated. Then, on the way to your ball, either walk around or step over the line leading from each ball to the hole.

If you step on someone's line, you create a concern that you have reduced his ability to sink his next putt. He doesn't need that psychological baggage and you don't need an enemy. So do the decent thing and be aware of those ball paths and spryly step over them.

Eyes On the Prize

This is it. This is the payoff for everything else. All the tee shots, the rough, the lost balls and OB, the bunkers, and everything else is all endured just to get here—to the hole. Now don't goof it up!

We all know the difficulty of sinking a putt, but it would be more difficult if the edge of the hole was uneven and out of round. Putts that might end up as perfect birdies could catch that uneven edge and be hurtled off by some odd gravitational spin of Einsteinian proportions—or they might just lip out. But either way, you're not going to be happy if it could have been prevented.

And it can be prevented. Whenever you are around the hole, whether reaching for or replacing the flagstick, retrieving your ball or just walking by, always make sure you keep your feet away from the hole. Everyone in every group behind you will be grateful, even though they did not know it was you who made that extra effort. They will benefit from your thoughtfulness and you will make the game better by your kindness.

Did You Know That?

You should never retrieve your golf ball from the hole by reaching in with the head of your putter and scooping it out. That could damage the hole. Remove the ball with your hand.

Rally Round the Flag

Like a beacon on a hill, the flagstick, flapping in
the breeze, beckons to us. From the tee it seems so
far away. Imagine: we have to get from here all the
way to there in just four swings of the club. That
seems impossible. But now you've made it. You're
on the green, ready to putt, and the flagstick is
within your grasp. But don't grab it just yet. There
are some important considerations regarding the
flagstick that you need to know as you wend your
way around the golf course.

In or Out?

A ball comes in from 150 yards, bounces twice on
the green, and bang, hits against the flagstick and
drops into the hole. Eagle! What a thrill.

When a shot comes in like that from off the green
and hits the flagstick, it's a perfectly legal shot.
The same is true if your ball is sitting anywhere off
the green, even right on the apron. Any shot that
starts from off the green can come into contact
with the flagstick and there is no problem.

So if someone in your group has a lie somewhere
off the green, he has a choice to leave the flag in
or take it out for his next shot. And you will be the
one who has to take it out for him, so remain alert
and ask what his preference is regarding the flag.

The choice to leave the flag in or take it out
depends largely on personal preference and the

circumstances of the shot. Some golf experts recommend leaving it in for all short shots around the green on the chance that a ball coming in too fast will hit the flagstick and be stopped. Meanwhile, they believe, no shot will be negatively influenced by the flagstick. In the end it always comes down to the preference of the golfer hitting the shot.

Tending the Flag

Once you are on the green, the rules change. A ball that is hit from on the green may not touch the flagstick, whether the flag is being tended or whether it is in the hole. So there are several things to consider in following the rules and applying the proper etiquette related to tending the flag.

If all golfers in your group are on the green and can see the hole adequately, then the flag does not need to be tended. The proper procedure is to remove the flagstick and lay it aside.

Did You Know That?

You should never drop the flagstick onto the green. The apparatus that attaches the flag to the stick can slam into the green and damage the grass (and that's a bad thing). So take a few steps and gently lay the flagstick off to the side of the green where it will not cause any damage.

There may be a number of reasons why someone in your group needs to have the flag tended, but generally it all boils down to, "I can't see the hole." And if she requests that the flag be tended, it is your responsibility to do it in a way that provides her the greatest opportunity to sink the putt without any concerns for lurking penalty strokes.

Tending the flag is simple, and is a skill that every golf enthusiast should master. I was taught by an excellent golfer when I was a young caddy. Here is the way it should be done:

- Grasp the flagstick with your arm outstretched to your side; that way your feet and body will be away from the hole.
- If you can reach it, hold the material of the flag against the stick to keep it from flapping in the breeze.
- Stand on the side of the hole that will allow your shadow to be cast away from the hole and the line of the oncoming putt.
- Gently remove the knob from the bottom of the cup so it does not get stuck when you are trying to pull it out. (Remember: if the ball hits the flagstick while you are fumbling to remove it, the golfer will get a two-stroke penalty and you will lose a friend.)
- Now, the most important part—become invisible!
- After the ball is stroked, remove the flagstick from the hole and move away from the hole, being careful not to step on the line of any other ball yet to be played.

- If no one else needs the flag tended, gently lay it off to the side of the green until it is replaced in the hole after everyone is done.

The entire group shares the responsibility of tending the flag. But in order to execute with the greatest efficiency and help with your pace of play, the person whose ball is closest to the hole should offer to tend the flag for the others. By the time they have all putted up, it is very likely no one else will need the flag tended.

Furthering Your Education

Somebody, who is a much better putter than me (which doesn't narrow it down very much), once said that all putts are straight putts. Obviously the comment was intended to demystify the concept of putting. But when you analyze the line of your putt, you can tell it rarely goes straight. There are twists and turns and things that go bump in the night that can influence the path of a putt. So any knowledge or insight you can gain that provides some advantage is welcome.

Since the rules of golf dictate that the one who is farthest away goes first, it sometimes works out so there is a player who must putt before you and right down the same line on which you will be putting momentarily. Well, no matter how experienced you are at reading putts, there is nothing quite as helpful as seeing, with your own eyes, exactly what is going to happen to your ball.

The Words and Wisdom on Golf

It's so bad I could putt off a tabletop and still leave the ball halfway down the leg.
—J C. Snead on his putting

That knowledge and confidence will give you just what you need when you stand over your putt—knowledge and confidence. So the natural thing to do is *go to school* on someone else's putt.

The education you receive from watching someone else's putt, however, must be balanced against your responsibility to extend an advanced degree of golf etiquette to the person putting. And that means you cannot just camp out on the extension of her putting line and wait to see how the ball travels to the hole.

What you can do, though, is wait until she has stroked her putt, then move quietly into position to see the ball travel to the hole. As a result, you may miss some of the action, but you will certainly see the most important part, which is how the ball breaks as it approaches the hole. And in the meantime, you have done your duty as an excellent golfer. Remember, it's for the good of the game—not *your* game, *the* game.

The Least You Need to Know

- Repair your ball mark and a couple of others that you see on the green.

- Mark your ball with a coin or token behind the ball before you pick it up. If asked to move your ball, mark it and then move the mark; when replacing it, move the mark back and then place the ball down.

- Don't touch the line of your putt in any way that will influence the path of your ball; however, you may repair ball marks, remove loose impediments, and remove movable obstructions.

- Walk around or step over the ball path of others in your group. Keep your feet away from the hole so you don't damage the structural integrity of the hole.

- If someone's ball is off the green, he has the option to leave the flag in or take it out. Learn the proper technique for tending the flag: don't drop the flag onto the green, place it gently off to the side.

- Before you "go to school" on somebody's putt, wait off to the side where you will not be a distraction during her stroke; move into position on the line after the ball is on its way to the hole.

Getting Down to Business

In This Chapter
- Why business and golf make sense
- Playing business golf
- Corporate and charity golf events

There are many good reasons why golf and business have forged such a firm bond throughout the history of these two important enterprises. It is more than just getting paid to be out in the sunshine for hours in the middle of a workday—charging the beverage cart on your expense report and playing a game you love—while your colleagues are slaving away in a dank and dingy office doing your paperwork under bad fluorescent lighting. Though, at the moment, that does seem like quite enough.

There is also the ability to develop important business relationships and further the goals of your company's long-term strategy and … did I mention charging the beverage cart to your expense report? In any event, let's look at some of the great reasons why your company should foster an enthusiastic participation in the world of business golf.

Business and Golf: The Perfect Twosome

It's a jungle out there! But that doesn't mean the laws of the jungle are the ones that will get you to your goal the fastest. In fact, it may be quite the opposite if the particular jungle you inhabit is the world of business.

You see, "civilization" is our attempt to replace the laws of the jungle with something that incorporates the contributions of more than just those with the biggest fangs or sharpest claws. And when civilization is functioning at its highest level, the thing that makes it operate most efficiently is our highly developed code of "etiquette."

At first glance this may seem contradictory to the old notion that "money makes the world go round," but it's not. Money still does make the world go round, but etiquette lubricates the wheels and eliminates the friction that would otherwise bring the whole thing to a grinding halt.

In many ways, the goals of the business golfer and the business practitioner are exactly the same. In order to understand the basic goals of the typical business executive, let's examine the typical company's mission statement. Then we can see how the overlay of business and golf is the perfect match.

When distilled to its purest form, the mission statement consists of the following components (usually lined up in this order):

- Provide the greatest value in our products/services
- Adhere to the highest ethical standards
- Treat our co-workers with respect
- Contribute to the well-being of our community
- Achieve the greatest return to investors

At their very essence, those are the same principles that form the foundation of good golf and good golf etiquette. Let's examine these concepts closely to see how the principles parallel one another in business and in golf.

Provide the Greatest Value in Our Products/Services

Creating the greatest value does not always mean providing the best product or service that is available. It implies a balance between the quality of the product and the price the marketplace is willing to pay for the product. Therefore, both JCPenney's and Nordstrom's can boast they are the best value (best products at their price-points).

The Words and Wisdom on Golf

If you watch a game, it's fun. If you play it, it's recreation. If you work at it, it's golf.
—Bob Hope

In golf, business people are constantly forced to choose between playing the kind of golf we would like to play and the game we are forced to play, given that we have to balance our golf practice time with working at our jobs and occasionally visiting our families. So instead of playing "high-quality golf," we play "high-value golf." ("Since I only get to play every other weekend and I don't even get to take one practice swing between rounds, an 89 is not a bad score. Hey, let's see Tiger Woods do *that!*")

Adhere to the Highest Ethical Standards

There are basically two places where the ethical standards of a company can be judged—in their policies and in their practices. In the not-too-distant past one could easily observe moral breaches in the general policies of many companies (e.g., in their hiring practices or in their approaches to environmental issues). But due to certain social reforms and pressures, it is now much less likely to find overall corporate policies that do not articulate squeaky-clean policies in most regards.

Any problems, therefore, must reside in the implementation of these policies by individuals who may be trying to promote their own personal agendas—agendas like getting bonuses or promotions. When people put their own advancement ahead of that of the company (often referred to as "greed"), the company suffers.

Golfers often face similar challenges when keeping
score (the golfing equivalent of the bottom line).
It's hard to imagine a golfer who has an overall
policy of cheating or wantonly violating the rules
of the game. In fact, most who love the game pro-
fess the greatest respect for and strictest adherence
to the rules. Yet there are often times when people
rely a bit too heavily on the "foot mashie" or the
mulligan to advance their own personal agendas—
like maintaining an impressively low handicap.

Did You Know That?

In a survey of business executives con-
ducted in the mid-1990s by an international resort company, 99 percent of the
executives surveyed described themselves
as being honest. However, 55 percent
also admitted to committing at least one
act of cheating, such as "moving a ball for
a better lie," "not counting a missed tap-
in," "intentionally miscounting the score on
a hole," or "secretly dropping a new ball
while looking for another one." Hmmm.

When golfers try to put their own needs ahead of
those of the game itself, it is the game that suffers.
Business people and golfers, however, who adhere to
the highest ethical standards are the ones who com-
mand the greatest respect from their colleagues.

Treat Our Co-Workers with Respect

A company is a community of people, hopefully working toward a common goal. If you want to motivate people to their highest level of productivity, there is no better way than to treat them with respect. By providing employees with safe working conditions, clear expectations, and reasonable rewards for their efforts, the community, as a whole, can prosper.

Companies that understand the benefits of helping and supporting one another to accomplish their common goals demonstrate respect for all employees regardless of their level within the organization. And people have proven over and over that when treated with respect and given the opportunity, there is no goal that cannot be achieved.

The Words and Wisdom on Golf

Golf is the only sport that a professional can enjoy playing with his friends. Can Larry Holmes enjoy fighting with one of his friends?

—Chi Chi Rodriguez

In golf, Rule 10 dictates the order of play. On the first tee, the order of play is determined randomly (everyone has an equal opportunity). After everyone has teed off, the order of play is determined by who is farthest from the hole. By letting the player who is "away" hit first, golfers keep the group moving ahead at the same pace, and they provide safety to the group by not letting some players get out in front of those who are hitting.

But most importantly, they show respect for those who are struggling within the group. The group does not abandon the poorest players to be picked up by another foursome coming up behind them. They recognize that all players within the group have value and are welcome.

On each new tee, the person who had the best score on the previous hole hits first, which is referred to as having the honor. In this way, golfers recognize outstanding performance. Rule 10 is based on the same concept used by a company that provides a mentoring program for new workers and has a "President's Club" for its top performers.

By respecting the needs of each participant, the community is stronger and the overall goals are met, whether it is in business or in golf.

Contribute to the Well-Being of Our Community

Companies that understand their commitment to the community in which they reside are revered by their neighbors. They participate in the community because they realize their kids will one day inherit their community and they want it to be someplace worth having.

Good golfers also appreciate the fact that they play golf in a beautiful environment, and in order to keep it beautiful each golfer must contribute. When golfers hit a shot from the tee or fairway and they dislodge a divot, they know it is their responsibility to replace or repair that divot. If a mark is made as a ball hits the green or as a golfer hits out of a bunker, the good golfer immediately repairs the mark so no one who comes behind will have to putt over an uneven surface or land in a footprint or blast mark in the bunker.

Why? Because those golfers know others will inherit the course after them and those who come behind are entitled to find the course in its original, pristine condition. Respect for the environment and the community demonstrates an advanced sense of responsibility for both the company and the golfer.

Achieve the Greatest Return for Our Investors

When all is said and done, business is about providing a return. But there should be more of a return than simply money. I have worked with a number of people who are well past the point of needing any more money. They are wealthy beyond most people's wildest dreams, yet every day they show up for work.

In fact, they don't just "show up," they come in with a tremendous enthusiasm for the day ahead. The reason they do is because they get a bigger return than just money.

The Words and Wisdom on Golf

We tournament golfers are much over-rated. We get paid too much.

—Tom Watson

Sure there are some people who think that business is just a bunch of cut-throat, greedy money-grabbers, and if that is your view, the business world would certainly be a terrible place to spend your life. But many whom I know are drawn to the constant challenges, the thrill of overcoming defeat, and the exhilaration of success. They understand and love the nuances of the game.

Golf is the same. For some, it seems like a meaningless, exasperating exercise—Mark Twain's "good walk spoiled." But for those who recognize the rhythm and the subtleties of the game, the history, traditions, and the rich lessons of life that can be learned from golf, the returns are plentiful and there is no game like it.

Love the Perks!

If your job provides you the opportunity to take clients, prospective customers, or fellow employees out to play golf, consider yourself among the very fortunate. While you are shepherding the development of meaningful business relations on behalf of your company, many of your co-workers are forlornly sitting in cubicles or hunched over desks wishing they were you. On the other hand, if you are being courted out on the golf course by a business associate for purposes of increasing business, as a candidate in a job interview, or simply to explore future possibilities, you are faced with an exciting, perhaps critical, opportunity and it is vital that you perform well.

Performing well in a business-golf situation is different than you might think at first. It does not mean you have to play great golf. In fact, the quality of your golf is much less important than your understanding of the surroundings and what is happening around you.

In order to make the outing as productive as possible, it is important that you understand the basic principles of business golf. The many tomes that have been written about conducting effective business golf can essentially be boiled down to three basic principles that you need to remember.

The three principles of business golf are atmosphere, relationship, and opportunity. If you can manage those three principles to your advantage, then every round of business golf you play will result in outstanding success.

Let's look at those three principles and explore the best ways to capitalize on those important rounds of business golf.

Atmosphere

The atmosphere you should be striving to achieve, whether you are the host or the guest, is one of fun, congeniality, and professionalism.

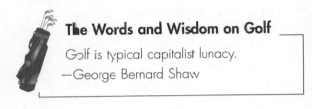

The Words and Wisdom on Golf

Golf is typical capitalist lunacy.
—George Bernard Shaw

In order to accomplish your goal, here are a few key points to remember:

- Dress—Standard golf attire is assumed, but as the host you should inform your guest if there are any special requirements regarding dress (e.g., no shorts).

- People—Make sure you have invited the right people to the event; they should be compatible and integral to accomplishing any goals you have set.

- Competition—If you wish to set up a match, keep it light and friendly and play for fun stakes (drinks after the round, or something innocuous like the title of "Best Golfer in the Universe"). Here is a place where that handicap will come in very handy. Also keep winning in perspective, play your best, but don't be overly competitive in a petty way.

- Attitude—Keep the round light but professional; avoid foul language, bad tempers, and crude jokes.

- Camaraderie—Be supportive and positive throughout the round; teasing and ribbing regarding someone else's game can easily get under the skin of another player and sour the day and any chance of advancing your cause.

Keeping the atmosphere positive and professional will lead to a successful day and the likelihood of repeat performances.

Relationship

At its very core, successful business is all about building relationships. And business golf is an excellent way to nurture and personalize those relationships for your own enjoyment and for the benefit of your business.

The Words and Wisdom on Golf

Eighteen holes of match or medal play will teach you more about your foe than will 18 years of dealing with him across a desk.

—Grantland Rice

More and more often, people are realizing the value of playing golf as a business tool, and nowhere is that more apparent than among female business professionals. Long excluded from the ranks of business golfers, women are finding that the links can provide a productive and lucrative venue for developing effective business relationships.

Whether you are an experienced business golfer, or new to the idea that golf can enhance your bottom line, it is important to understand what the relationship is all about out on the links. Consider the following points to support your efforts at building relationships through golf:

- Golf etiquette is much more important than your ability to swing the club; go back and review all of the important golf-etiquette tips in the earlier chapters, especially those on pace of play.

- Understand and play by the rules. People who don't play by the rules will not be seen as good partners in business. Never cheat or bend the rules to your advantage, but also don't be too hard-nosed about enforcing the rules on others.

- Know your game and play your game. Lose the old stereotype that you shouldn't beat the boss; for the most part, business people are grown-ups and if you're a good golfer, it will be fun to watch you play well.

- Ask questions about your colleague's family, hobbies, other interests, or travel; pick up on leads for conversations regarding common interests; it may be wise to avoid the killer topics like politics or religion for now.

- Be yourself and have fun; that's what building relationships is all about.

Golf is full of ups and downs. We all know that it can be exciting and rewarding, but it can also be frustrating and aggravating—from one shot to the next. How you deal with all those situations on the course will provide great insight into what kind of person you are and how you will handle those same situations in a business setting. Think about that before you tee off in that round of business golf. The kind of person you are will certainly be on display, and it will influence the relationships you develop through golf.

The Words and Wisdom on Golf

The only way of really finding out a man's true character is to play golf with him. In no other walk of life does the cloven hoof so quickly display itself.

—P. G. Wodehouse

Opportunity

The "opportunity" is the bottom line. Business may be all about relationships, but those relationships are designed to translate into benefits for the enterprise. And there is nothing wrong with that. Every businessperson understands the responsibilities that lead to success.

A nuance of the business round of golf that must be kept entirely in perspective, however, is that this is still golf. And the reason golf has been chosen as the venue in which to nurture this relationship is because of the mutual passion for the game as well as the passion for succeeding in business. Therefore, an unspoken balance is struck that encourages the personal side to flourish and the game to be played and appreciated to its fullest, but "businessy" things like the "terms of the agreement" and the "start date" can be left for another time.

Did You Know That?

At many of the most elite country clubs, including Augusta National, members are prohibited from discussing business on the course.

Think of the strength you project as a businessperson if you show up to play golf with a prospective partner and you adopt the attitude that this is just you and me, person to person. Everything else can wait. That takes confidence.

The opportunity is what the game is all about, but the subtlety of the situation dictates that you demonstrate restraint regarding conducting business on the course. There are some tips on how to handle the opportunity.

- Be a good listener. If your partner brings up the business issues, be prepared to respond, but don't lead the charge to bring up business topics.

- Take advantage of any chance to follow up golf with dinner or drinks, where business issues may be brought up freely.

- Use the day as the lead-in to future meetings to discuss the business details.

- Be prompt with a thank-you note and reciprocal invitation, if that is appropriate, and use that as an entrée to more discussions.

The daily grind of the business world can be a stressful environment in which to ply your trade. Getting away from it all, while still advancing the cause, is the perfect solution and that is the whole point of business golf. If you have not figured out the advantages yet, it's time to jump in with both feet—just be sure to wear soft spikes.

Giving 'Till It Hurts

Throughout your corporate career you will be faced with many opportunities to play golf at a company event or in a charity tournament. Those events provide you with a chance to represent your department or project; your company; and, most importantly, yourself. Don't pass up the occasion to advance your career, and don't miss the rung on the ladder that comes with effective networking; it will enable you to grow professionally and to impress your colleagues.

Corporate Golf

An important point to remember in corporate golf is that you are not necessarily showing off your skills at golf, you are showing off who you are as a person. Therefore it is, once again, wise to go back and review the earlier overview of golf etiquette and rules.

If you can't knock the ball right down the middle in an outstanding display of power and control, then at least don't slow the whole thing down by making everyone play at a snail's pace. Remember, there is usually a really good dinner at the end of a corporate or charity event, and everyone wants a good seat at the table.

Here is the really good news for nongolfers who get roped into playing in a corporate or charity golf event: they usually play a "best-ball" format. Best-ball means that after each golfer has hit a shot, you all go to the place where the best shot landed and hit your next shot from there.

So you get to pick up your lousy shot, make a few jokes about the next time you play in the U.S. Open, and drop it right where the studly intern from Stanford Business School hit his. And here's the best part: you keep one score for the entire group. Cool!

The bad news is that best-ball tournaments usually require each group to use at least three tee shots from every golfer. That will probably mean that after your group plays 15 holes and they are now 15-under because they have been able to chuckle past your game all day, you will hear a loud "group gulp" as you approach the sixteenth tee and all eyes are fixed on you. No worries. Just don't hit one in the lake.

Here are some thoughts to help you get through the traumatic, career-making (or career-breaking) round of corporate golf:

- If you are a new golfer, take a lesson or two before the event. If you're experienced, go hit a few buckets as a tune-up.

- Be sure you have the right equipment: decent clubs, extra golf balls, tees, etc. And carefully review the earlier chapters on golf rules and etiquette.

- A very positive attitude goes a lot further than a tossed golf club, so keep it light; a little self-deprecating humor sprinkled in can make the day a big success, especially if you are playing with people who are lower on the org chart than you.

- Most importantly, have fun; that is what corporate events are all about.

Playing golf with your colleagues is a wonderful way to build camaraderie with the people in your company. And if you rely on your "secret weapon," you will never have to worry about the level of your golf skills. The secret weapon that you can rely on in any golf event to make you look like an insider is nothing more than knowing golf etiquette. Master the golf etiquette and you will be welcome in any foursome.

Charity Golf Events

One of the most remarkable facets of the game of golf is its ability to generate significant amounts of money for worthwhile charities. Not only do the PGA and LPGA provide millions of dollars for a wide variety of notable causes, but local charity events also raise countless millions every year for everything from cancer research to the neighborhood kid who needs some help with medical bills.

Here are a few ways for your company to become involved in the community, get some visibility, and contribute in a way that can make a difference in the lives of real people:

- Become a sponsor at a charity golf event. You may not be able to sponsor the entire event, but you can sponsor a hole, a dinner, the hole-in-one contest, or for the greatest visibility, the beverage cart.

- Donate prizes or auction items such as your own products or services, a week at your vacation home, a family outing in your boat, or anything you can think of that will help raise money for the cause.

- Encourage your employees to join charity golf events as foursomes; it will give your company very positive visibility within the community.
- Pledge to match the funds raised by a certain aspect of the event, for instance, all the money raised by the "mulligan fees."
- Recruit the local high school golf team to be caddies in the charity event, and have your company donate $50 for every caddy who participates. That way, you help raise money, you provide a unique experience for the golfers, and you teach the kids the value of contributing to the community while demonstrating their passion for golf.

There are so many ways to make golf an effective strategy for enhancing your business that you are only limited by your imagination. (That's not a problem, is it?) Make sure your organization has a strategy that includes the many benefits of business golf.

The Least You Need to Know

- Business and golf are a perfect match because the values that are integral to both activities are so similar.
- Business golf is about the atmosphere, the relationship, and the opportunity. Be sure to consider all three as you plan your business-golf strategy.

- Your attitude and behavior on the course will be much more important than your actual golf skills in representing your company, so sharpen your golf etiquette skills as much as your golf skills.

- Charity golf events are a great way to reward and support your own team and they provide a valuable link to your community as well. Participate as often and as generously as you can.

Chapter  **9**

The Rule Book: Grip It and Rip It

In This Chapter

- Help from Mr. Mulligan
- Gimme some love
- Various and sundry others

When you play on the PGA Tour, the rules of golf become a part of your inner psyche. You probably wake up at night in a cold sweat, wondering if your arm was perfectly level when you took that last drop or whether you broke the rule about accepting advice when you had a conversation on the green with your imaginary friend. But when you play golf with your buddies, things are different. The sun is shining, the beer cart is driving in your direction, and suddenly the rules of golf become somewhat of an afterthought or, at the very least, the subject of idle speculation.

Let's face it, when you go out and play touch football, you don't spend a lot of time worrying about the backfield being in motion or the slightest movement of the offensive line. Of course, you'll observe the agreed-upon lines for out of bounds and the goals, but you're looking to have some fun, and a rigid adherence to the rules isn't necessarily a part of it. It's the same thing when you go out to have a casual round of golf with the "buds."

I know it can be tempting, on a really bad day, to take a totally new approach to golf and say, "Let's see who can get the ball into the hole in the *most* strokes." But really, what are the rules that you can "overlook" when you're playing a casual game that don't count? Well, the answer is probably "all of them." But there would be a point at which your activity would stop resembling golf. So let's look at a few of the rules that can be glossed over when you are just playing for fun.

The Golfer's Little Helper

Probably the second-most-often uttered phrase on the golf course, right after, "Hey, did you guys see where my ball went?" is the very famous, "Would you mind if I take a mulligan?" And, interestingly enough, those two phrases very often follow about that closely.

No one knows for sure the origin of the term "mulligan," but every golfer appreciates its rich meaning. The mulligan is golf-speak for a free do-over. Right after you have drastically flubbed a shot off the tee, nothing restores a golfer's equilibrium like a well-struck mulligan right down the middle.

But before you get too cozy with your new friend, here are a few things to keep in mind regarding the use of the "Divine Mr. M."

- First off, don't overdo the mulligans; when mulligans are used, a generally accepted limit is imposed. Usually it is agreed that there will be one mulligan allowed off the first tee (just to avoid the "first-tee jitters"), or one on the front and one on the back. But other than that, play it as it lies.

- Mulligans should only be requested/granted when you are on the tee—there is no such thing as a mulligan out of the fairway or out of a hazard.

- Hit your mulligan after every other player has hit a first shot.

- If you think you might have the occasion to hit a mulligan, now and again keep a ball in your pocket so you don't hold everyone up while you fumble through your bag for another.

- If you are not playing with a limit on mulligans, remember the groups behind you. They might get a bit impatient if you are hitting mulligans on every hole and slowing down the pace of play.

- If you take a mulligan on every hole, don't brag around the clubhouse about how you broke 90. You may find it hard to find a playing partner the next time out.

The mulligan is certainly here to stay. Almost every golfer has taken a mulligan at one time or another. It can be a great way to forgive a bad shot, especially when you are first learning the game. And every once in a while it's nice to be able to say to a friend in need, "Hey, why don't you take a mulligan." As long as it's every once in a while.

In the Leather

The closest cousin to the mulligan, a freebee off the tee, is the *gimme*, which is a freebee on the green. The gimme does two things. First, it can help to speed up play by not requiring the golfer to line up, set up, and stroke the last putt. Second, and most importantly, it takes the pressure off the golfer to sink a little putt that should be automatic (but sometimes isn't).

The term "gimme" is a corruption of the request to "give me," as in, "Will someone give me this putt?" The standard by which an acceptable gimme is determined is if the golfer is *in the leather*. The expression "in the leather" has nothing to do with the undergarments being worn by the golfer; instead it refers to a measure of distance. If you place the head of your putter in the hole and lay the putter flat on the green toward the ball, the ball should be within the distance from the hole to the point on the putter shaft where the grip begins.

In the old days (up through the 1920s) golf grips were made of leather, so the phrase was easily recognizable. But with the modern evolution of belly putters and forehead putters and pole-vaulting putters, the term may have lost some of its significance (but it certainly allows for longer and longer gimmes!).

Did You Know That?

In the year 1457 the Scottish Parliament of James II banned golf and football (that is, soccer), because they interfered with military training for the wars against the English. The ability to play was reinstated in 1502 after the signing of the Treaty of Glasgow between Scotland and England.

When you're playing golf with your buddies, the gimmes can flow like beer, but here are a few things to think about regarding gimmes:

- You should never give someone a gimme for a birdie; some things still need to be earned.
- If someone offers you a gimme, and you accept it, you should pick up and move on. If you attempt the putt after the gimme has been offered and you miss the putt, you should take the extra stroke.
- Remember: a gimme still counts as a stroke. The benefit you are getting is the removal of the possibility of missing the putt, but you still have to account for the stroke it would have taken to get the ball into the hole.

Gimmes are a vote of confidence from your friends and a wonderful innovation in the game of golf. As long as you keep them in perspective and don't go to the well too many times, they make the game go more quickly and they add an element of fun and grace. Wouldn't it be great if there were a lot more places in life where we could get gimmes?

Observing the Rules from a Distance

Obviously, we all have the greatest respect and devotion to the rules of golf. Right? (Wink, wink, nudge, nudge.) But every once in a while, isn't there a fleeting moment when you hold that rule book in your hands and you'd like to finally put that old John Daly phrase to good use, "Grip it and rip it!"?

Well, here are a few rules that you can enjoy overlooking when you're just playing for fun.

OB (Stroke and Distance)

Okay, so you've hit one that started leaning toward the fence but it was unclear whether it went OB. You forgot to hit a provisional ball, and while you are walking to your ball, you discover that without a doubt, it has landed out of bounds. What to do, what to do?

Well as you now know from reading the previous chapters of this book, you need to go back and hit another ball and do the whole stroke-and-distance thing. But that would require a rather long walk and a lot of time, so here is a shortcut you can take:

drop a ball within a club length or two of where you went out, count a penalty stroke, and count another stroke for the distance (so you lie 3).

That would be the equivalent of hitting another ball to the exact same spot, but saves a ton of time. And the good news is, you get the extra penalty of being in a lousy spot, so you can feel like you are really doing your part to sort of observe the rules.

Did You Know That?

Golf balls were originally crafted of wood, but in 1618 the golfing world was introduced to the "featherie" golf ball. It was a leather sphere stuffed with a top hat full of chicken feathers. Unfortunately, it was expensive to manufacture (sometimes more costly than a golf club), so that put them out of reach for the general playing population. In 1848 the mass-produced gutta-percha ball was introduced, and that opened the game up to a broader spectrum of society.

Ball in Front of the Tee Markers

Placing your ball on a tee in between the markers that are clearly visible and are there specifically to define the teeing area seems somewhat like a simple task. But believe it or not, you will occasionally see someone tee up her ball several inches in front of the tee markers. In fact, I once played with an experienced golfer who, for no apparent reason, got up on the fifteenth tee and teed up his ball a good two feet in front of the markers.

When that happens it is pretty unlikely the golfer was trying to cheat and get an advantage of a couple of inches (or even a few feet). In fact, it's a fairly good bet the golfer was so deeply entrenched in sorting out the eighteen conflicting swing thoughts swirling through his mind, that he had no idea it was even his turn to hit.

The Words and Wisdom on Golf

Excessive golf dwarfs the intellect. Nor is this to be wondered at when we consider that the more fatuously vacant the mind is, the better for play. It has been observed that absolute idiots play the steadiest.

—Sir Walter Simpson

Now according to the rules of golf, that infraction would be worth a two-stroke penalty. But we all know there are some infractions that come with a far greater penalty than mere strokes—and being stupid in front of your friends is definitely one of those infractions. In fact, not assessing the penalty is a far crueler punishment since it sends the pitiable message, "We understand you're not bright enough to follow this simple rule, so we'll let you slide."

If you play your cards right, the guy will end up begging for the two-stroke penalty—but don't let him off that easy.

Improving Your Lie

As was amply noted earlier, the things you cannot improve during play are your stance, area of intended swing, line of play, or your lie. Well that seems like an awful lot to remember, especially if you're inclined to break all of those rules on one shot.

Did You Know That?

The term "bogey" as used in golf was originally borrowed from a popular British song in the late nineteenth century. In the song, the Bogey Man sang, "Catch me if you can." So bogey was originally used to designate a good score (something that people sought after) and was synonymous with "par." But later (early twentieth century), as "par" came into more common usage to designate the standard score for a hole, "bogey" was reassigned to the role of one over par.

Here is an area, actually four areas, where you can cut some slack to a friend who is experiencing problems with his game. Let's face it, if your friend has hit into a jungle and he's trying to salvage a "Hail Mary" shot out of the deep undergrowth all the way up to the green, the last things on his mind are stance, swing, line, and lie. He's much more concerned about gators, snakes, quicksand, and finding his way back to the golf course.

So if he decides to throw some logs down to stand on, trims back a few branches to clear his backswing, bends a few trees to provide an opening for his shot, and peels back some palm fronds to get at his ball, forget the penalty strokes—this guy deserves a merit badge!

Too Many Clubs in the Bag

Golfers are allowed to have no more than 14 clubs in their bag during a round of golf. But the number 14 is a fairly arbitrary choice. During the 1920s and 30s many pro golfers played with over 20 clubs in their bags. The number 14 was chosen in 1938 because it corresponded to what was considered a standard set of clubs at that time.

But what happens if, during your round of golf with a friend, the friend discovers that his teenage son has been using Dad's clubs and placed too many clubs in the bag? Should the father be penalized two strokes? This is an age-old question in society: should the father be punished for the transgressions of his son?

Before we can really answer that question, we must remember that the Rules of Golf are supposedly based on the principles of equity. Therefore we can clearly see that this father should be allowed to deduct two strokes for raising a teenager who puts things back when he is finished with them.

Of course, this would be a rare occurrence, so it won't affect the rules of golf very often.

But the important golf principle to remember is to never let your kids mess around with your clubs.

The Words and Wisdom on Golf

Golf is the only game in which a precise knowledge of the rules can earn one a reputation for bad sportsmanship.

—Patrick Campbell

The Least You Need to Know

- Mulligans should be used only sparingly. Keep a ball handy in case you need to hit one, and wait until everyone has hit a first shot before hitting your mulligan.

- Mulligans are only acceptable after a tee shot, never from the fairway or other area of the course.

- Gimmes are granted only for close putts, generally those "in the leather." A gimme still requires you to count the stroke that would have been taken to sink the putt.

- Whenever you play a round that will be calculated into your handicap, you need to adhere to the rules of golf, but when you are just out messing around with your friends for fun, it's okay to take a little leeway with the rules—as long as it doesn't affect the pace of play.

Glossary

90-degree rule A cart rule designed to reduce wear and tear on fairways. Motorized carts remain on the cart path until even with the location of your ball in the fairway; the cart then turns 90 degrees and drives out onto the fairway to the ball; after the shot is played, the cart returns directly to the cart path and proceeds to the next shot.

address the ball Taking a stance in preparation for a shot; includes grounding the club (except in a hazard where grounding the club is prohibited).

area of intended swing The area that will be used by the golfer to swing the club back and forward in an attempt to stroke the ball.

at the turn Between the front and back nines; at the end of the ninth hole, before the tenth hole.

ball in play See *in play*.

ball picker Cart used at practice ranges to retrieve golf balls from the field.

build a stance Improving upon the natural footing at address of the ball in order to get a better position from which to stroke the ball.

bunker A hazard on the golf course that is filled with sand; golfers often refer to bunkers as "sand traps," but that term is not used in the Rules of Golf.

cart path only A cart rule designed to protect vulnerable fairways. When the course restricts carts to cart path only, you may not drive your cart onto the fairway, and must walk from the cart path to your ball for your shot.

casual water A temporary collection of water on the course from which a golfer is entitled to free relief.

closely mown area An area of the golf course that is mown as closely as the fairway or shorter.

dance floor A slang term for the "green."

divot The clump of grass and dirt that is removed from the ground when a golfer hits a shot. The term is also used interchangeably to refer to the hole that is left when that piece of sod is vacated.

double hit A single swing on which the golfer contacts the ball two times.

drop The act of letting a golf ball fall to a spot on the ground designated by a golf rule.

embedded ball A ball the has lodged into the ground as the result of landing in soft earth after a shot.

fore The term shouted by golfers to warn others that a ball is heading in their direction or some other danger may be present.

free relief   The ability to move a ball away from interference without a penalty stroke.

from the tips   A slang term meaning the golfer is playing from the tee boxes that are farthest to the back; these golfers are playing the longest layout provided on the course.

gimme   A courtesy putt that is allowed to a golfer in a nontournament situation without the requirement to actually putt it. The stroke that would have been taken is counted in the score. Gimmes are only used for short putts (see *in the leather*) and are outside the rules of golf.

go to school   Watching the path a ball takes to the hole after it has been stroked by a player who is putting prior to you and along the same or similar path that you have to putt.

golf etiquette   The traditional set of rules that are observed among golfers to reinforce the courtesies and practices necessary for each golfer to play his or her optimum round of golf.

Golfing Gorilla   The world-famous golfing primate who is often seen performing his long-drive skills and a variety of human tricks at charity golf events.

ground under repair (GUR)   An area under temporary construction or development that is designated by the grounds crew as ground under repair. Golfers are allowed a free lift out of areas designated as GUR.

grounding your club in the hazard Touching the golf club on the ground while the ball is in an area marked as a hazard.

handicap The USGA system of rating a golfer's ability according to a formula based on a number of factors including scores, number of rounds played, difficulty of courses, etc. The handicap number issued to a golfer indicates the golfer's potential score for a round of golf (e.g., a 10 handicap would likely shoot 10 over par).

hazards Areas of difficulty on the golf course designated by the rules for special consideration during play. Generally they include bunkers (a.k.a. sand traps) and any areas designated by red or yellow stakes or lines.

honor The privilege of hitting first based on the fact that you achieved the best score on the previous hole.

immovable obstructions Various artificial objects or surfaces that may impede a golfer's line, lie, stance, or swing. Because these obstructions cannot be moved, golfers must play around them.

in play A ball is said to be "in play" after it has been intentionally hit from the tee and until it falls into the hole. A ball may be legally taken out of play under certain rules.

in the leather A measure of distance from the hole to the point on a putter where the grip begins when the head of the putter is in the hole. This measure is used to determine whether a gimme is grantable or not.

line of play The direction the player wishes the ball to take after the stroke, including a little bit to each side of that line and the vertical space above it. On the green the line of play is along the ground.

lateral water hazard An area on the golf course designated by red stakes or red lines.

lift Picking up a golf ball that is in play, with the authorization of a golf rule.

local rules Additional rules of play that apply to the specific golf course on which a golfer is playing; local rules must be authorized by the USGA.

loose impediment Natural objects such as stones and twigs lying behind or around a ball that may prevent the golfer from making clean contact with the ball during a stroke.

lost golf ball A golf ball that cannot be located after a search of no more than 5 minutes.

lost outside of a hazard A golf ball that cannot be located after a search of no more than 5 minutes that is not in an area designated as a hazard.

marked Before a ball may be taken out of play, the spot it occupies must be marked according to the rules so the ball can be replaced to the exact same spot.

movable obstructions Various artificial objects such as waste paper baskets, litter or benches that may impede a golfer's line, lie, stance, or swing. Movable obstructions may be moved out of the way without penalty.

mulligan An extra tee shot, which is not counted in the score and which is taken after one's first tee shot is poorly executed. Mulligans are outside the Rules of Golf.

nearest point of relief The closest spot on the golf course that is away from interference where a player may drop or place a ball when complying with a golf rule.

OB An abbreviation for "out of bounds."

order of play The order in which golfers take their turns to hit.

orthodontist Someone who straightens your kid's teeth two days a week and plays golf five days a week.

pace of play The tempo of a round of golf; ideally a round should take between 4 and $4\frac{1}{2}$ hours to play.

penalty stroke An extra stroke that is added to the score of a golfer who has committed an infraction of the Rules of Golf.

placing the ball Putting the ball in a specific spot designated by the Rules of Golf.

play it as it lies The most basic rule of golf, which tells golfers that they must play the ball as they find it, regardless of how much they want to improve the lie before they hit it again.

play through Passing a slower group or individual on the golf course.

plumb-bob Determining the likely break of a putt by suspending your putter vertically in front of the line and eye-balling it for a considerable amount of time.

practice range What some people call the driving range, but because you do more than practice "driving" there, it makes more sense to call it the practice range.

previous hole placement The circular scar on the green that is left over after the previous location of the hole is filled in when the grounds crew makes a new hole.

provisional ball An extra ball that is allowed by the Rules of Golf in case the first ball hit by the golfer might be lost. Hitting the provisional ball saves time since the golfer would have to go back and hit a second ball in the event the first ball is determined to be lost or out of bounds.

ready golf The system used by golfers who wish to play a quick round of golf whereby they abandon the standard rules of order of play and allow whoever is ready to play next.

re-drop Dropping a ball again if a ball has been dropped according to the rules but it does not come to rest in a place allowed by the rules.

red stakes (or red lines) Markers designating a lateral water hazard on a golf course.

sand divot The blast mark left in the sand after a golfer has taken a shot in a bunker.

stymie A former rule of golf under which a ball on the green blocked another ball from getting to the hole. The blocked player was required to putt over or around the stymie. That rule is no longer played, as players now mark balls on the green allowing all golfers direct access to the hole.

stroke and distance A penalty for out-of-bounds or a lost ball under which the golfer must hit again from the same spot in addition to counting a penalty stroke.

swing plane The angle created by your posture and arms at address, and as that angle proceeds through your backswing and your forward swing, the angle of the arc of your swing (for more details ask a PGA teaching pro).

teeing ground The official place designated for taking a tee shot; located in the rectangle that is created by the tee markers and a distance of two club lengths back from the front edge of tee markers.

tee boxes The general areas provided by the golf course for purposes of taking tee shots; usually divided into at least three separate areas for a front tee, middle tee, and back tees. Grounds crews will move the teeing ground to different spots within the tee boxes.

test the conditions Trying to determine how a shot will play by using your hands or feet, by rolling a ball, or some other method before hitting the ball with a stroke.

"thru the green" (through the green)   The entire area of the course except the teeing ground, the green to which you are currently playing, and any hazard on the course.

tee time   The reservation that you set up to establish your appointed time to play golf.

tending the flag   The golf-etiquette courtesy of holding the flagstick so another player can adequately see the hole while lining up and executing a putt.

unplayable lie   A determination made by a golfer that the ball is in a spot from which it cannot be hit.

USGA   The United States Golf Association. The USGA is the governing body that articulates the rules for play in the United States, its territories, and Mexico. Visit www.usga.org for complete information.

water hazard   An area on the golf course designated by yellow stakes or yellow lines.

whiff   An intentional swing at the ball without making contact with the ball (swing and a miss).

white stakes (or white lines)   Markers designating the boundary of the playable area of a golf course. Beyond the white stakes or lines is out of bounds.

wrong ball   A ball that is played by a golfer other than that golfer's official ball in play.

wrong green A green on the golf course that is not the green to which you are currently playing, but where your ball has nonetheless landed.

yellow stakes (or yellow lines) Markers designating a water hazard on a golf course.

yips A mental affliction that affects golfers, causing them to lose confidence in their putting skills. The yips can cause head jerking, wrist snapping, shoulder twitching, and knee rattling. Other symptoms include purchasing several new putters and several new styles of putters—all in the same season.

Articles and Laws in Playing at Golf

The game of golf, as we know it today, rose up from very humble beginnings. Tradition tells us that a few shepherds in the hills of Northern Scotland created the game by hitting rocks into rabbit holes using their shepherd crooks as clubs. Then over the decades and centuries that followed, the game, the equipment, and the golf courses evolved into the modern game of golf.

By the year 1457 golf was so popular it was banned in Scotland because it interfered with the practice of archery, which was vital for the national defense. But despite the restrictions put on the game by the government and the church, people played it anyway (some things never change). With the Treaty of Glasgow in 1502, the ban was lifted. Then James VI of Scotland took a liking to the game, himself, and golf was firmly established.

The Gentlemen Golfers of Leith formed the first golf club in order to support an annual golf competition. The club was later renamed The Honourable Company of Edinburgh Golfers and in 1744 they established and formalized the first set of rules for the game of golf.

Here are the original rules of golf, as hand-written by the Honorable Company of Edinburgh Golfers in 1744. The use of capital letters and misspelled words are retained here for historical flavor.

1. You must Tee your Ball within a Club's length of the Hole.

2. Your Tee must be upon the Ground.

3. You are not to change the Ball which you Strike off the Tee.

4. You are not to remove Stones, Bones, or any Break Club, for the sake of playing your Ball, Except upon the fair Green and that only within a Club's length of your Ball.

5. If your Ball comes among watter, or any wattery filth, you are at liberty to take out your Ball & bringing it behind the hazard and Teeing it, you may play it with any Club and allow your Adversary a Stroke for so getting out your Ball.

6. If your Balls be found any where touching one another, You are to lift the first Ball, till you play the last.

7. At Holeing, you are to play your Ball honestly for the Hole, and not to play upon your Adversary's Ball, not lying in your way to the Hole.

8. If you should lose your Ball, by its being taken up, or any other way, you are to go back to the Spot, where you struck last, & drop another Ball, And allow your adversary a Stroke for the misfortune.

9. No man at Holeing his Ball, is to be allowed, to mark his way to the Hole with his Club, or anything else.

10. If a Ball be stopp'd by any Person, Horse, Dog or anything else, The Ball so stop'd must be play'd where it lyes.

11. If you draw your Club in Order to Strike, & proceed so far in the Stroke as to be bringing down your Club; If then, your Club shall break, in any way, it is to be Accounted a Stroke.

12. He whose Ball lyes farthest from the Hole is obliged to play first.

13. Neither Trench, Ditch, or Dyke, made for the preservation of the Links, nor the Scholar's Holes, or the Soldier's Lines, Shall be accounted a Hazard; But the Ball is to be taken out teed and play'd with any Iren Club.

John Rattray, Capt

Amendment to the Articles & Laws—1758

The 5th, and 13th Articles of the foregoing Laws having occasioned frequent Disputes It is found Convenient That in all time Coming, the Law Shall be, That in no Case Whatever a Ball Shall be Lifted without losing a Stroke Except it is in the Scholars holes When it may be taken out teed and played with any Iron Club without losing a Stroke—And in all other Cases the Ball must be Played where it lyes Except it is at least half Covered with Watter or filth When it may, if the Player Chuses be taken out Teed and Played with any Club upon Loosing a Stroke.

Thomas Boswall, Capt

Index

THE COMPLETE IDIOT'S GUIDE TO

"Michelle is interested in teaching you the basics of the golf swing, but her first goal is to help you enjoy yourself out on the golf course."
—Dave Stockton, winner of 11 PGA Tour and 14 Champions Tour tournaments

Golf

SECOND EDITION

- **Detailed photos** from top instructors to help you master swing, technique, and more
- **Easy-to-understand basics** from tee shots to putting essentials and even specialty shots
- **The lastest info** on rules, course strategy, fitness, equipment, technology, and more

Michelle McGann, LPGA tour member, and Matthew Rudy, *Golf Digest*

ISBN: 978-1-59257-309-7

A how-to-golf guide that will suit you to a "tee"

- Expert advice and practical tips on how to improve all aspects of your game
- Easy-to-understand instruction on deconstructing and mastering your swing
- Essential strategies for playing different holes
- Practical routines for fitness and gym workouts that will keep you limber and injury-free

idiotsguides.com